To the congregation of The First Assembly of God in Kelso, Washington, with whom I have already shared these glorious truths.

LIVING BY FAITH

Don Mallough

GOSPEL PUBLISHING HOUSE
SPRINGFIELD, MISSOURI
02-0552

Library of Congress Catalog Card Number 77-91484
International Standard Book Number 0-88243-552-3
Printed in the United States of America

Contents

Prologue

A basic rule of interpretation is that any document must be its own interpreter. Surely that is true of the Bible. How it interprets itself is a key to understanding its message. New Testament writers often quoted from the Old Testament. How they, under inspiration of the Spirit of God, interpreted those events gives us a path into a thorough understanding of the truth. We learn from them what is important and what is not. That which is exemplary is stressed while the opposite is condemned. Observing the interpretive methods of the New Testament writers enables us to be competent expositors of the Scriptures ourselves.

Hebrews 11 presents the most complete treatise of faith to be found in the Bible. It starts with a description and then proceeds to give biographical illustrations of real faith in action. The roll presents some great surprises. In some instances it is because of who is selected but more often because of the episodes chosen to illustrate faith. The actions involved were anything but conventional. Faith was the moving force by which a dead man was made to speak, another just disappeared from the earth, a landlocked amateur carpenter built a boat, a solid citizen became a nomad, a 90-year-old woman gave birth to a child, a godly man volunteered to commit murder, and a prince gave up the palace to become a sheepherder.

By faith the weirdest battle strategy conceivable was planned and executed. A governmental leader who was experiencing every good thing life could afford had faith to believe that things were going to get worse. Faith even brought a "scarlet" woman into the lineage of our Lord, to the chagrin of all the purists. For some, faith brought great deliverance but for others it only gave grace to endure suffering, poverty, and affliction while they were living in dens and caves. The experiences are varied and the actions most unusual.

In this book we will fall into step with the interpretations and emphases of the writer of the Epistle to the Hebrews. We will tread old paths and new. Hopefully, we will come to a better understanding of faith and what made these unusual events such great examples of that mighty force. The material presented here is in no way exhaustive. My basic hope is that it will pique your curiosity to pursue a more intensive study of faith with a view to putting its dynamic power to greater use in your life.

Don Mallough

1

The Significance of Faith

> Now faith is the substance of things hoped for, the evidence of things not seen. For by it the elders obtained a good report. Through faith we understand that the worlds were framed by the word of God, so that things which are seen were not made of things which do appear.
>
> Hebrews 11:1-3

Faith honors God and God honors faith. There are many ways of pleasing God but all involve faith. We are explicitly told, "Without faith it is impossible to please him" (v. 6). From that statement it is evident that the more one exercises faith the more pleasing it is to the Lord. Faith brings all the resources of God into play and that alters every viewpoint and prospect.

Hebrews 11 is the great "faith chapter" of the Scriptures and has often been called God's "hall of fame." The word *faith* (or its substitute pronoun) appears 26 times within the chapter. The writer of this Epistle, as inspired by the Holy Spirit, focuses on the exploits of faith and we shall do the same on these pages.

This chapter begins with the best single description of faith available to us. It could be called the divine description. Many and varied are the attempted definitions but they succeed in presenting faith in only a limited aspect or just one of its many facets. The dictionary makes an attempt but it still falls far short of the full meaning. It calls faith a firm belief in something for which there is no proof. Actually, faith *is* the proof. Faith is substance. It is the evidence. The Berkeley translation expresses it this way: "Faith forms a solid ground for what is hoped for."

Some other translations use the descriptive compound word *title-deed.* That brings to mind a picture of something tangible to assure us of a reality that has not come into the range of our natural vision. *The Amplified New Testament* expresses it as "perceiving as real what is not revealed to the senses." Faith is a power by which the unreal becomes real. It does for the unreal what reason does for the real.

Of course, the faith of which we speak, and which is cited in this chapter, is a faith in God. Faith standing alone is nebulous; it must be anchored to something or someone. Our faith lays hold on God and in that way brings His unlimited power into play. Dr. M. R. DeHaan gives a definition that stresses faith's relationship to God and His Word: "Faith is believing the unreasonable, the impossible and the unexplainable because someone else, in whom we have absolute confidence, has said it was so, and upon His word we believe it without asking any further proof." H. C. Benner says: "Faith is that attitude of heart and mind that brings God into the situation." When God is involved the whole picture is changed.

Faith is the vital element in a life that pleases God. It is the principal ingredient in any formula of success. Faith is a means of knowledge (v. 3), a medium of power (v. 11), and a producer of action (v. 7). It imbues one with a daring and venturesome spirit (v. 8). It is a versatile implement that makes it possible for a mere man to perceive the invisible, believe the incredible, and achieve the impossible. What a power is at our disposal!

Faith provides us with a penetrating perception. By it we are able to understand certain facts that somehow elude the most brilliant intellects. An example is given here in the reference to the creation of the universe. A casual reader assumes that the worlds were formed by faith (v. 3), but that is not what it says. It is by faith that we *understand* that fact.

Reason may lead us astray but faith brings us directly to the Creator. Scientists and philosophers search in vain for the true origin of the universe if they eliminate God and follow their pursuits without faith. They may produce hypotheses and educated guesses but it ends there. It isn't that faith makes true what is patently false, but rather that it zeros in on the true and then provides the ability to comprehend it.

The Phillips translation stresses this point: "And it is after all only by faith that our minds accept as fact that the whole scheme of time and space was created by God's command—that the world which we can see has come into being by principles which are invisible" (v. 3). *The Twentieth Century New Testament* sums it up: "Faith enables us to perceive that the universe was created at the bidding of God." Hence, faith is an asset in our research and not a liability.

Faith in God is in no way inconsistent with the search for scientific facts. Rather, it is a helping hand. The late Dr. Wernher von Braun, for many years the director of the Marshall Space Flight Center in

Huntsville, Alabama, attested to that truth. He said: "Without the recognition of Divine Intent, the developments in the animate and spiritual worlds simply cannot be understood." When addressing The International Christian Leadership Conference in Washington, D.C. he declared: "We should remember that science exists only because there are people, and its concepts exist only in the minds of men. Behind these concepts lies the reality which is being revealed to us—but only by the grace of God."

In an interview with C. M. Ward, Dr. von Braun dispelled the prevalent idea that science and faith are on a collision course by saying: "I know of no scientific discovery that would necessitate a change of relationship between God and man. The farther we probe into space the greater is my faith."

Whether or not we can adequately define faith, it is possible to demonstrate it. Someone in another generation has said, "I cannot explain the wind but I can hoist a sail." The writer of this Epistle gives us the best description of faith he can fashion and then cites examples from history in which faith played a prominent role. That is the essence of this great chapter. Even the most perfect definition tends to leave us cold and unmoved. As we review these exploits of faith, however, we are challenged to venture out for God as did these illustrious worthies of the past.

It is important to us that such a variety of persons and experiences are inscribed on this roll of honor. Faith is operative in people from different generations, backgrounds, and life-styles in diverse situations. Faith enabled these individuals to worship, walk, build, venture, anticipate, give birth, die, sacrifice, foresee, choose, forsake, remember, attack, befriend, and, not least of all, suffer. This makes it natural for us to identify with at least one of the persons in this chapter. Do we have any problem or precarious situation that does not find a kinship to at least one item on the above list? By having a practical example of exercising faith in a comparable situation we are challenged to respond in a similar manner.

Not one of the persons in this gallery was perfect. This is not an honor roll of perfection. No claim is made that all their actions were exemplary or to be commended. No stamp of approval is put on all they did. And they did not always demonstrate the same degree of faith in their other experiences. Some showed little faith prior to or following their exemplary experiences mentioned here. They were men and women of manifold imperfections. Very few, if any, had plans or strategies that could stand the test of sheer logic or conventional procedure.

In spite of all this, they pleased God. It was their faith that produced the smile of God's approval. Faith in God was the one thing they had in common. The instances chosen from their lives for Hebrews 11 are the mountain peaks of faith. God's evaluation is not the same as ours. We are in for some great surprises as we examine closely these great experiences of faith.

2

A Voice From the Grave

> By faith Abel offered unto God a more excellent sacrifice than Cain, by which he obtained witness that he was righteous, God testifying of his gifts: and by it he being dead yet speaketh.
>
> Hebrews 11:4

Faith enables a man to speak eloquently even after he has been dead for a millennium. Lips that have been silenced for multiplied centuries still convey to us age-old truths about man's relationship to God. From the first grave that was ever dug comes a message that directs our approach to God.

It is deeply significant that the very first household was divided on the matter of religion. Not only that, but the division resulted in a catastrophe—the murder of an innocent person. As inconceivable and illogical as it may seem, history's pages are blotched with blood because of religious differences in the family of man. Armies have marched to war waving banners declaring their religious beliefs and have justified their butchery in the name of their faith. Our astonishment at such tactics can best be understood by knowing what brought about the cleavage between the first brothers, Cain and Abel.

Because these brothers were part of the first family

and lived during the infancy of the human race, many of the incidents in their lives provide a series of firsts for mankind. In Genesis 4:1-8 we see fallen man's first approach to God and his attempt to worship Him; the first recorded instance of a sacrifice being offered to Jehovah; the first time a sinner was accepted by God and the first time one was rejected by Him; the first death, the first murder, and the first martyr for truth. Those few verses present a microcosm of human approaches to God and their results, both good and bad.

Cain and Abel were much alike and started out on common ground. Both of them were sinners, both were sincere, both wanted to please God, and both brought a sacrifice that was convenient for them. Cain, being a farmer, brought produce from the ground and Abel, being a herdsman, brought a young lamb from his flock. With so much in common it would seem logical that the results of their approach to God would be the same. However, surprisingly, they were very different. God smiled on Abel and was very pleased with him. This is what Abel had sought and he was very gratified with the results. On the other hand, God frowned upon Cain and made it quite evident that He was not pleased with him. This infuriated Cain and prompted him to take some very strange actions.

Why was God's attitude so different toward these two who had so much in common? Is He partial? Does He capriciously express a like for one person and a dislike for another? Are men to be continually plagued by the puzzling actions of God in accepting some men and rejecting others? What was the reason for God smiling on Abel and frowning on Cain?

If sincerity were the basis for acceptance by God

then Cain would have qualified for His blessing. If merely bringing an offering were the requirement then he would have met the test. If one can claim to be right with God just because he is as good as his brother then Cain had a strong case to argue. If, as some people say, "The only thing that matters is that we worship the same God," then he could say that and feel smug and complacent. The truth is that none of these claims were of any help to him, nor are they to us today. God had rejected him and no one knew it any better than Cain did. The reason God rejected Cain is still the basis for the rejection of his posterity.

As God viewed it, the difference was not in the two men but in the sacrifices they brought: "By faith Abel offered unto God *a more excellent sacrifice.*" God accepted Abel because of the qualities of his gift and rejected Cain because of the deficiencies in his. The sacrifice of Abel was more acceptable than that of Cain. Both brothers approached God by means of a sacrifice. Hence, the difference lies in the manner of approach to God. The acceptance or rejection of the man himself is determined by his means and attitude in approaching God. The hopes of each man were centered in the sacrifice by which he came to God. What was established as a principle in that ancient time is still true today. By what means and upon whose merit we come to God is the determining factor in whether or not we will receive His smile of approval.

Just what significant qualities made the difference between Abel's sacrifice and Cain's? One cardinal element in Abel's gift was missing in the offering of Cain—the shedding of blood. Before a lamb could be offered as a sacrifice to Jehovah, it must be slain and its blood shed. Right at the beginning of the human race God was establishing a principle that was to be known and adhered to by sinful man. Shed blood was to be a prerequisite for man's approach to God. The blood of an innocent lamb was to be shed for the sins of a man. It is God's declaration that the blood makes atonement for the soul (Leviticus 17:11). If there is no shed blood there is no forgiveness of sin (Hebrews 9:22). In his unforgiven state sinful man has no access to God.

All of this foreshadowed the shed blood of Jesus Christ which purchased atonement for us and thus access to God (Ephesians 2:13; Hebrews 9:14; 1 Peter 1:19; 1 John 1:7). Abel showed a clear perception of true atonement in bringing a sacrifice that was preceded by shed blood.

The sacrifice of Cain, although offered with every good intention, lacked the important factor of shed blood and that is the basic reason why it was rejected by God. It was also deficient because it was made up of the fruit of a cursed ground. When man initially sinned, God had said: "Cursed is the ground for thy sake" (Genesis 3:17). Now Cain offered produce from that cursed ground in an offering unto a holy God. Is it any wonder God frowned on that sacrifice and the man who was putting his whole trust in it to bring him the blessing of God?

Not only was the ground cursed at the fall of man but the flesh was as well. Paul testified: "In my flesh dwelleth no good thing" (Romans 7:18). God himself associated the cursed ground with the extreme wickedness of human beings in their sinful state (Genesis 8:21).

Many men try to seek God's favor by offering Him the good works of their lives. They assume that by such a display of goodness they merit the smile of

God. Our Lord is just as adamant in rejecting such an offering as He was in spurning the sacrifice of Cain—and for the same reason. No matter how appealing, good works are offered without any blood atonement and are the fruit of a cursed ground.

If God had accepted Cain's sacrifice, to be consistent He would have had to accept any sincere offering of man, even the fruit of a cursed ground. He refused to do this when the very first sacrifices were offered and He still maintains that attitude today. God rejected Cain and his sacrifice and He does the same for those who approach Him in a similar way. He accepts and smiles on all who come trusting in the blood sacrifice of Jesus Christ and His merits alone.

The attitude of Cain toward his rejection is most revealing. Common sense would have told him that the difference lay in the type of sacrifice offered. Even after that, if he had brought an offering of a lamb, as did his brother, he would have experienced the smile of God. It was as simple as that. God reminded him that if he did the proper thing he would be accepted but if he didn't then sin would take over (Genesis 4:7).

Cain's reaction was the opposite, however. Sin reared its ugly head in his life. He allowed resentment to build up within him against both God and man. Instead of experiencing the sweet forgiveness of God, a hatred for Him boiled and festered within his breast. It took the outward form of animosity toward his own brother Abel, who had done nothing to deserve his wrath but was to bear the awful brunt of it. One day when they were walking together in a field, Cain took a blunt instrument and hit Abel on the head and killed him. Thus, the first murder was spawned out of a religious cleavage in the first human family.

Barry and Garry Thompson had a very happy boyhood. They were exceptionally close to each other, as are most twins. During their last year in high school Barry met Vesta and a romance blossomed. She took him to a small church that she attended and he accepted Christ. Later they were married and established a happy Christian home.

All these developments affected his brother Garry adversely. They tried to lead him to Christ but he would have none of it. He became sullen and rebellious about many things. He looked upon his brother as a competitor instead of his twin and life-long companion. He blamed Vesta for coming between them. His sour attitude entered into all his other activities. At the least provocation he would argue and quibble. He thought he was always right and everyone else was wrong. Friends wondered how twins could be so different.

It wasn't Vesta or their marriage that changed things for Garry. It was the more important event that happened about the same time. By faith Barry came to Christ and became a new person. Garry could have had the same experience but flatly refused it. Like Cain, he lived with a chip on his shoulder—to his own detriment.

Faith, or the lack of it, can make a vast difference between any two persons—even identical twins.

Out of this Biblical incident in early human history the basic principle of religious persecution was forged and it prevails right down to the present day. Those who have a form of religion with no evident power or blessing are the most likely candidates to administer persecution. When such persons see the evident blessing of God upon others and the lack of it in their own lives, they stoop to carnal means to persecute those who are the recipients of God's blessing. Cain slew Abel for that reason. The same thing happened in the crucifixion of Jesus Christ and in the martyrdom of Stephen. Thus it has always been and always shall be.

Cain, the rejected sinner, thought he had solved his problems in one fell swoop. With Abel dead, there would be no one to remind him of his deficiencies before God; therefore, he wouldn't feel inferior or guilty. The experience of the contrasting sacrifices could be buried in the debris of the past. He could assert himself as being as good as anyone and no one could contradict him. How foolish was his reasoning and that of men in all ages who have behaved like him. Murder only added to his guilt. The lips may have been stilled in death but Abel went on speaking in posthumous eloquence that reverberates even in the 20th century.

How can a man speak after he has been dead for 6,000 years? Abel does so by an example of faith during his brief lifetime. He preaches in the stentorian voice of example and it is conveyed to us on the pages of the Scriptures. By faith, Abel approached God through a vicarious sacrifice made possible by the shedding of blood. By that approved approach he forcefully tells all men that they too can obtain peace with God by trusting in the blood sacrifice of Calvary.

3
A Unique Life

> By faith Enoch was translated that he should not see death; and was not found, because God had translated him: for before his translation he had this testimony, that he pleased God.
>
> Hebrews 11:5

> And Enoch walked (in habitual fellowship) with God; and he was not, for God took him (home with Him).
>
> Genesis 5:24 *(The Amplified Bible)*

Perhaps the best account of the unique life of Enoch is that given by a young lad who had just returned from Sunday school. When asked about the day's lesson he said: "Enoch and God went for a walk. They went on for a long time and then God said, 'Enoch, it's getting late and we're closer to my house than to yours. Why don't you just come home with me?' "

The most startling aspect of Enoch's life on earth was the way it ended. It is his translation that captures our fancy and makes the name of Enoch stand out in history. It was the climax of a refreshingly different life of faith and was brought about by the power of faith. With a dull monotony the chronicles of human activities end with "and he died." Then this sparkling jewel among genealogies tells of a triumphant life that bypassed the portal of death enroute to the glory world.

In other ways Enoch's life was also different. It was brief in spite of the fact that he lived 365 years. Length of life is comparative. We would count 365 years as a very long life but when compared to that of his contemporaries it was very short. His father Jared lived 962 years and his son Methuselah lived 969 years. Only two other men listed in Genesis 5 lived under 900 years and each lived more than twice as long as Enoch. By that standard he was just a young fellow when he departed this life.

The heart of this brief biography is found in the four words, "Enoch walked with God." That sentence speaks volumes. The importance of his walk is stressed in the fact that it is mentioned twice in the original account (Genesis 5:22, 24). There is a strong intimation in the first of these two verses that he only started his walk with God about the time his son Methuselah was born.

Men do not instinctively live the consecrated life. It usually starts with a crisis experience. This is definitely true in the Christian era and in the teaching of the gospel. The apostle Paul had just such an experience on the road to Damascus. He later referred to it as a pattern or example of what a real conversion should be (1 Timothy 1:16). He also alluded to the revolutionary effect of such an experience in enabling one to begin his walk with God (2 Corinthians 5:17).

To walk with God sounds very simple. In a sense it is difficult and yet in another way it is easy. Enoch demonstrated that it is possible to walk consistently with God and be pleasing in His sight even amid wicked surroundings and among godless companions. If he could do so in his day it is possible for us to do the same in ours. It was Enoch's faith that sparked his good life, made possible his exemplary walk with God, and eventually brought about his translation.

This matter of walking with God involves much that is not always evident on the surface. For this reason such a simple statement as, "Enoch walked with God," tells much about his unique life. Let us pause to consider the various facets of such a walk that make it intriguing and inspiring. By doing so we can understand what it meant to Enoch, but more important, what such a walk means to us.

Walking with God involves acquaintance with Him. It is not only possible for us to be personally acquainted with God but it is necessary if we are to walk with Him. It is not sufficient to merely know about Him or to render lip service to the fact that He exists in some distant place. "Acquaint now thyself with him, and be at peace: thereby good shall come unto thee" (Job 22:21). The accusations Eliphaz brought against Job may not have been justified but his advice in this verse is good for anyone.

Walking with God involves an intimacy with Him. Such intimacy develops as the walk progresses. Familiarity and affection grow side by side. Through constant communion and social intercourse men take on the ways of each other. The assumption of each other's characteristics is not always equal, however. If one of the two partners is dominant, the other party tends to be influenced by him rather than to influence him. This was definitely true as Enoch walked with God and also as we do so too. When the Creator walks with one He has created, it is man who benefits because he takes on the ways of God. Walking with

God sets up that intimacy and encourages it as the walk progresses.

Walking with God involves going in the same direction and keeping step with Him. It was not so much that God walked with Enoch but that Enoch walked with God. Rather than God going Enoch's way it was Enoch going God's way. Someone once asked Abraham Lincoln if he thought God was on his side. He answered that far more important was whether or not he was on God's side. The initiative rests with us: "Draw nigh to God, and he will draw nigh to you" (James 4:8).

One cannot walk with God without walking God's way. Such a walk calls for a common purpose and direction. It demands a striding along together with no rushing ahead or lagging behind. A great secret in Christian victory lies in keeping step with God. When there is a constant, common gait; mutual sharing; and an identical goal, the fellowship is ideal.

Walking with God involves agreement with Him. The prophet Amos poses a question to which the answer is self-evident: "Can two walk together, except they be agreed?" (Amos 3:3). Harmony is essential to a consistent walk with two persons. When there is discord or disagreement that walk is disrupted. The apostle Paul describes the incompatibility when those with basic disagreements are yoked together (2 Corinthians 6:14-16). The fact that Enoch walked with God indicates they were in harmony with each other. It is possible for us to walk with Him and demonstrate that same harmony.

Walking with God produces spiritual progress. There is nothing spectacular about walking but it is surprising how much ground can be covered in that way. With just a uniform gait, even if it is termed "plodding," there is consistent progress and advancement. As one steadily walks with God he is better off with each passing day. More spiritual headway is made by unvarying strides than by running for a time and then stopping periodically. To the believers at Galatia who were mired in legalism Paul wrote: "Ye did run well; who did hinder you . . . ?" (Galatians 5:7) They had sprinted off to a great start but later had completely stopped. This happens all too often. Enoch walked with God with such regularity that it became the habit of his life. His was a consistent spirituality that was steadily increasing. May it also be so with us.

Walking with God produces a vibrant testimony. For 300 years Enoch bore witness to the existence of God and to the fact that men could have communion with Him. He knew God himself and thus he was an authentic witness. By spoken word and demonstrated life he made known to many the reality of God. He also made them conscious of God's presence. His testimony continues to bear fruit even unto this day.

More is involved in a testimony than mere words, no matter how fluent they may be. Our life must speak as loudly as our utterances. Behind both must be a vital experience with God. A personal knowledge of God, augmented by a consistent walk with Him, produces words that make a missionary impact on those around us. It is such a testimony that counts for eternity.

A few years ago a friend of mine, James R. Swanson, was visiting in Scotland. He made a special effort to go to a small town in the northern part of that country. His father, now deceased, had been born there and he wanted to see the area he had heard so much about.

He knew of no one to contact so he just walked around and visualized his father in that setting. As he came down a narrow street an old man sitting on a bench spoke up, "Excuse me, young man," he said, "But would you by chance be any kin to a James Swanson who lived in this village years ago?" When informed that he was his son the old gentleman said, "I could tell by your walk that you belonged to him."

Walking with God inevitably brings us to God's house. The ultimate goal of the child of God is to be in the house of God and with Him for all eternity. This holds no attraction for the unbeliever, but to those who have been brought into this fellowship by grace and love Him, it is a long-sought objective. Those who love God's house here (the church) and walk with Him daily, have a longing to be with Him where there will be no severing of the fellowship.

Not only is this the goal of the child of God but it is the prayer and expressed wish of our Saviour that it be so. Jesus prayed: "Father, I will that they also, who thou hast given me, be with me where I am; that they may behold my glory, which thou hast given me" (John 17:24). He also promised that this will come to pass: "In my Father's house are many mansions. . . . I go to prepare a place for you. And if I go and prepare a place for you, I will come again, and receive you unto myself; that where I am, there ye may be also" (14:2, 3). The Psalmist sensed that hope and exulted: "I will dwell in the house of the Lord forever" (Psalm 23:6).

The life of Enoch was unique and refreshingly different. It was not so different, however, that it cannot be emulated. Every experience that was his in that day of long ago can be ours today. Even the glorious climactic translation that makes his biography distinctive will be the experience of some of us. His being caught away and bypassing death was just a miniature demonstration of what will happen to all believers when Christ returns: "For the Lord himself shall descend from heaven with a shout, with the voice of the archangel, and with the trump of God: and the dead in Christ shall rise first: then we which are alive and remain shall be caught up together with them in the clouds, to meet the Lord in the air: and so shall we ever be with the Lord" (1 Thessalonians 4:16, 17).

May the Lord hasten the day when that most unique life of Enoch shall be so emulated as to make it commonplace.

4

How to Get Something From God

> But without faith it is impossible to please him; for he that cometh to God must believe that he is, and that he is a rewarder of them that diligently seek him.
> Hebrews 11:6

The benefits of faith are twofold. By it the heart of God is delighted and the persevering seeker is rewarded also. One such aspect is cited by example in the previous verse and a formula for the other is expressed in this one. True faith pleases God, seeks God, and receives bountifully from Him.

Continuity in this list of heroes of faith is briefly broken here. Alluding to a faith in Enoch that pleased God leads to the statement that only by faith can anyone please Him. Then the writer proceeds to give a practical how-to-do-it formula for reaching God, pleasing Him, and receiving something from Him.

Although the opening statement of this verse is negative, it presents a positive truth that is a cornerstone of the gospel. Gramatically, the double negative in the sentence makes it an emphatic, inescapable declaration. The little word *must* emphasizes that faith is imperative. It substantiates four basic conclusions and makes them irrefutable: (1) God is pleased with those who exercise faith. (2) To please God one must have faith. (3) No man ever pleased God without faith. (4) Without faith man cannot communicate with God, much less receive anything from Him.

A clinching argument from another portion of the Scriptures has to do with man receiving the salvation of God: "He that believeth on him is not condemned: but he that believeth not is condemned already, because he hath not believed in the name of the only begotten Son of God" (John 3:18).

To qualify as how-to-do-it instruction the steps and procedures must be explicit and simple. Nothing could be simpler than the four steps outlined in this verse. No one can read them and claim ignorance as to how to get answers to his prayers. Why should we make these matters mysterious and complicated when we have before us such simple instructions?

Nowhere does the Bible offer an argument for the existence of God. Not even in the prologue of Genesis is there a hint of one. Instead it laconically declares: "In the beginning God." There is no call for evidence that a Supreme Being exists. It is an accepted fact. It is more natural for a human being to accept the existence of God than to question it. The great struggle is with those who don't want to believe and attempt to summon arguments substantiating their own prejudices. There is a void within the human breast that cries out for God. Whenever civilized man has burst through the jungles and frontiers he has always found even the most primitive beings worshiping something. The object of their worship may be strange but they make obeisance to a god of some kind.

This is the first and simplest requisite in the process of getting something from God. It calls for believing in an unoriginated, self-existent Being who is infinite, eternal, and omnipotent. This step is essential but it is only the beginning.

Our basic responsibility is to come to God through Jesus Christ. Again we use the illustration of obtaining the greatest of all gifts from God—salvation. Jesus said: "Come unto me . . . and I will give you rest" (Matthew 11:28). On another occasion He charged that the reason good men did not possess eternal life was because they had failed to come to Him: "And ye will not come to me, that ye might have life" (John 5:40). By this statement He implied what the Bible teaches throughout: eternal life is to be had by coming to Him.

The gifts of God are not distributed promiscuously. He bestows them upon those who take the initiative and come to Him. Such coming is an outward manifestation of faith. Our sincere intention to receive must be laid on the line to start the giving process on His part. The requirement that we come to Him for salvation is the same as that for receiving anything from Him. This is the second step in the formula and indicates that He can be found.

Not only does the formula call for our coming to God initially but continuously. Our intensity and continuity in seeking Him has a bearing on the results. It is not a single process. It involves more than coming once and asking once. It calls for more than superficial action: "When ye shall search for me with all your heart . . . I will be found of you, saith the Lord" (Jeremiah 29:13, 14). That verse stresses the intensity of seeking Him while another Old Testament passage points out the matter of continuity: "As long as he sought the Lord, God made him to prosper" (2 Chronicles 26:5). The blessing of God in the life of Uzziah was contingent on his constantly being in the attitude of seeking God. What was true for him is equally true for us.

It is significant that we are admonished to seek *Him* rather than any particular gifts He may have to offer. His gifts and blessings come as we seek and commune with Him. We are to seek the Giver rather than the gifts and the Blesser rather than the blessings.

Even the appropriating of a just compensation calls for faith. God has made ample provision for many but the recipients are often few. Christ died for the sins of the whole world but all have not experienced saving grace. This is not due to a limit of supply or to God's reluctance to give. It is because men do not embrace the promises or take possession of what is provided for them.

To get something from God there is one step even beyond diligently seeking Him. It is to appropriate what God delights to give and what we would benefit by having. The reward may be available but until we accept it by faith it is not actually ours.

On several occasions when I have been teaching about a faith that appropriates I have demonstrated it in a simple way. From my pocket I extract a $1 bill. Then in a casual way I say, "This is a *bona fide* piece of American currency. I am going to give it to the first person who claims it." I do not hesitate at the end of the sentence but go right on talking.

The reaction is almost always the same. There is a slight stir among the congregation. Children look at one another laughingly and at their parents with a questioning glance. There is more whispering than usual. A gangly boy starts to get up but when there is a titter of laughter he sits down, afraid of being embarrassed. In the meantime I continue preaching on faith as if nothing unusual were happening. After what seems a long time someone will walk to the platform and put out his hand. I hand him the money and he returns to his seat.

After that demonstration it is easy to stress a faith that receives from God. Everyone heard my statement and each could put the dollar to good use. The people hesitated because it sounded too simple. Did I really mean it? Was there an embarrassing trick involved? Finally, someone came. He believed what I had said and came for what I had promised. So it is with the faith that appropriates the promissory utterance of God.

This very practical formula can be used in any aspect of our Christian living. As we follow these four steps we are able to receive from the Lord that which we need or would be beneficial to us.

5
Faith and Fear

> By faith Noah, being warned of God of things not seen as yet, moved with fear, prepared an ark to the saving of his house; by the which he condemned the world, and became heir of the righteousness which is by faith.
>
> Hebrews 11:7

In the life of Noah faith and fear worked in consort. These elements that seem so unrelated became partners in fulfilling God's plan for the human race. Two forces that are usually assumed to pull in opposite directions teamed up together to achieve a noble objective. Faith stirred the emotion of fear and good came out of it. This is an admirable demonstration of the fact that fear too can have an integral part in God's scheme of things.

Why is it so commonly assumed that other emotions can rightly move people toward God but that fear should play no such role? In other areas of life fear often motivates resolute action. Is there any reason it should not do so in the vital matter of man's salvation?

There are two facets of fear that we are admonished to exercise and use. One is a reverential fear of God and the other is the fear of impending consequences: "Let us have grace, whereby we may serve God acceptably with reverence and godly fear" (Hebrews 12:28). Then Jude tells us how we are to deal with the ungodly: "And of some have compassion, making a difference: and others save with fear" (vv. 22, 23). It was not the overwhelming sense of God's love that caused Noah to build that ark. It was the fear of the consequences if he did not do so. Faith believed God's warning and the fear of the coming deluge prompted him to do what was necessary to save his family.

In one sense faith serves as a telescope. It puts the unseen into our range of vision. That which is dim, obscure, and shrouded is brought into clear focus. It is through faith that we see, understand, and know that which was previously beyond our grasp. It is the instrument by which we are able to comprehend the thoughts and actions of God.

Noah must surely have been aware of the wickedness that prevailed in his world. With his natural eyes, however, he could not see the degree to which evil had saturated the lives of his fellowmen. The Lord saw conditions as they really were: "And God saw that the wickedness of man was great in the earth, and that every imagination of the thoughts of his heart was only evil continually" (Genesis 6:5). Could it be possible that *every* imagination was *evil continually?* This is hard to comprehend when one sees his fellowman from the exterior only. So often the facade of respectability does its intended work of prettying up the picture.

It was only by faith that Noah could see the gross wickedness of men. Faith in God allowed him to see the chaotic mess through the eyes of God. Because of this he didn't protest the prophesied flood that would destroy them all. That was the first part of what faith enabled him to see.

God was on speaking terms with Noah and chose to confide in him His plan to destroy most of mankind: "And God said unto Noah, The end of all flesh is come before me; for the earth is filled with violence through them; and, behold, I will destroy them with the earth" (v. 13). Faith brought Noah near enough to God to get the message and enabled him to believe it. He was able to visualize the catastrophic flood, although it was in the distant future and natural logic would contend that such an event could never transpire.

From the standpoint of natural reasoning a person would have been very gullible to believe there could ever be a flood. There was no precedent for such an event. Not only had there never been a flood, but it had never even rained! "For the Lord had not caused it to rain upon the earth . . . but there went up a mist from the earth, and watered the whole face of the ground" (2:5, 6). There was no evidence or indication anywhere that "the windows of heaven would open" and there would be a downpour for 40 days and nights. Only by faith could Noah envision, proclaim, and make preparation for such an event.

Not only could the natural eye find no precedent for a flood in the past, but in scanning the future there was not even the slightest indication of such a deluge. When the word reached Noah the flood was well over a century away. Only with the telescope of faith could it be brought into focus and confidently foretold.

God revealed the secret of impending judgment to Noah and Noah had faith enough to take Him at His word. Just how the Lord spoke to him we are not told. It is immaterial whether it was by a dream, vision, or audible voice. He who sits at the master controls of the universe unfolded His plan and immediately Noah's faith became operative, enabling him to see the predicted catastrophe as clearly as if it were happening then.

The vibrant faith of Noah was exemplary because it was accompanied by works. "Faith without works is dead" (James 2:20). He not only accepted and believed the message but acted upon it. He not only walked with God but worked with Him as well. His action in building the ark was the consummate expression of his faith.

Because of that faith Noah ventured into a gigantic task for which he had no experience. If he had laid himself open for ridicule by declaring an impending flood, he did so even more when he started building a boat on dry ground. The project was not even near a river, sea, or lake. The work was exacting, difficult, and messy and it seemed as if the job would never end. As the years passed there was more room for doubt and the taunting and jeering of his contemporaries grew louder and more exasperating.

There was no glamor in the work Noah was doing and yet every bit of it was a result of, and attested to, his faith. It was not a task of his own choosing but he willingly responded to the instructions from the Lord. Faith hears the still small voice even above the clamor and sophistries of fellow human beings. In this instance the sound of the hammer and adz were a reminder of one man's faith in God.

One day I left my office and went down into the basement of the building. I saw a frail-looking woman holding a board on a sawhorse with her knee and laboriously trying to saw off a piece of it. I recognized her as author Billie Davis. "Well," I remarked humorously, "It looks as if we have a new carpenter." "No," was her quick reply, "I am writing a book." Then she explained her statement. In her writing task of the moment she had suggested a how-to-do-it procedure for her readers. She had left her typewriter to try making the object herself to be sure it could be done.

Billie Davis was being very practical in writing a book with a hammer and saw. And it was a practical faith that prompted Noah to believe God's warning and build an ark when natural reasoning would say it was an act of folly.

Noah's deeds were not limited to carpentry, however. Peter characterizes this man of faith as "a preacher of righteousness." He not only believed God and demonstrated that belief in a practical way, but he also preached what his faith had embraced. The message God had imparted to him must be passed on to others. The urgency of impending doom made such preaching necessary. If he believed God's message then he could do nothing but prepare for the deluge and constantly exhort others to do likewise.

There was no gigantic ingathering of believers resulting from the preaching and example of Noah. No one has ventured to classify him as one of the world's greatest revivalists. Those who strongly stress visible results would probably count him as a good man—but more of a failure than a success. Yet, in spite of that, he is listed here in God's hall of fame with the great of all the ages. This is another example that God's evaluation differs from that of man. We tabulate statistics and make awards to the highest total. God's gauge measures faithfulness and His accolades often go to those in the shadows of human obscurity.

Although not spectacular, there were definite results to Noah's ministry. First, he was saved himself and by his faith he "became heir of the righteousness which is by faith." This is the first objective of faith and should in no way be minimized. One thing is certain, without faith it couldn't have happened.

Then, because of his faith and its evidence, members of his own household were saved. This too was no mean accomplishment. Some have been faithful and labored long and have not seen such results. Seeing seven persons saved who would otherwise have been lost was well worthwhile. The very fact that they were members of his family gave even a greater sense of satisfaction.

These seven members of his family did not depend only on Noah's faith. They had faith of their own as a result of his demonstration of confidence in God. When they entered the ark there wasn't a cloud in the sky and the rain was still 7 days off. They too must have had faith in God's promises to have made that move.

The third result of Noah's faith is most puzzling to the casual reader. The writer says: ". . . by the which he condemned the world." What a strange result that is! How did he do it? Wasn't the world already condemned when God imparted the secret of coming judgment? Just why should such condemnation be counted as an accomplishment?

By Noah's faith, preaching, and example the people were told the truth about their future. The message was more than a tormenting threat. It brought them hope for salvation through the ark. It was not merely a negative message of impending judgment but held out hope if they would believe and act.

Some of us misunderstand the motives of God or

His servants in sounding a note of judgment. We are prone to think of Him as sadistic and cruel to torment mankind with such harsh pronouncements. The truth is that it is God's loving mercy that prompts such warnings. If He delighted in punishing men He would wreak judgment on the world without warning.

Both God and Noah were responsible for holding out hope to individuals in an already condemned world. Then, if they would still be lost they would reap condemnation by their own deliberate acts. He gave them a chance to be saved, so the responsibility for their fate would rest on their own shoulders. It is in this sense that the faith of Noah condemned the world. Although it is a negative and calamitous action it resulted from that faith. Men died without God and with sneers and laughter on their lips, but not without having had a chance to be saved. That generation was held accountable because it had heard Noah's words, witnessed his example, and was keenly aware of his faithfulness.

Noah had faith in God, fear of the coming deluge, and hope for salvation. He followed God's plan for his own salvation and for those who would exercise a similar faith.

6
Sealed Orders

By faith Abraham, when he was called to go out into a place which he should afterward receive for an inheritance, obeyed; and he went out, not knowing whither he went. By faith he sojourned in the land of promise, as in a strange country, dwelling in tabernacles with Isaac and Jacob, the heirs with him of the same promise: for he looked for a city which hath foundations, whose builder and maker is God.

Hebrews 11:8-10

In times of war or national emergency it is not uncommon for a ship to sail out of port under sealed orders. At the time of departure no one on board, including the captain, knows the destination or the route of the vessel. Only after they are at sea are the orders opened and read.

There is a sense in which Abraham left his ancestral home in Ur under such sealed orders. This was a part of his colorful and adventurous life of faith.

Abraham holds a unique position in this gallery of the faithful. More is recorded about his faith than that of any other person. Almost a third of the chapter deals with his exploits. Even in the Genesis account much space is devoted to the record of his deeds and accomplishments. No other individual received as many personal promises from the Lord or so demonstrated an ability to believe and base his life upon them. Is it any wonder he is called "the father of the faithful"?

How astounding was the decision of Abraham! Who would leave his kindred, home, and country with so little regard for the consequences? Who would make a decision affecting his whole pattern of living with so few facts at his disposal? The list of unknown factors and uncertainties was long and formidable. He did not know the name of the land to which he was going or in what direction he would travel. His route was completely unknown to him and he had no idea where the land was or how far away. He had no way of knowing what its pertinent features were. What about the terrain, topography, climate, and living conditions?

He didn't even know if it would be a better or more beautiful area. We refer to it as a "land of milk and honey" and speak of how much better it was than Chaldea. However, what we know now in retrospect he did not know—even by intimation. God just said: "Get thee out . . . unto a land that I will show thee." That could be good or bad, he knew not which. Technically, he did not even have a promise of a deed to the land. God had merely said He would show it to him. The writer of the Book of Hebrews ascribes it as "a place which he should afterward receive for an inheritance," but that was written after the events were history. Abraham didn't even have that assurance when he made his decision.

Not only were there few facts to lure him on this long journey but there were no real reasons for leaving his home city. He had in no way grown discontent. There was no famine or poverty to prod him to look for greener pastures. His family did not suffer persecution or undue hardship. This critical move was not the result of burning ambition on Abraham's part or self-will that made him fly in the face of all that seemed proper and right to do. By all processes of logic there was no reason for his seeking a new home or for leaving the one that he had.

If one were to list the pros and cons in making the decision that faced Abraham it would be a lopsided record. All the accepted points of reasoning would be stacked against his making a move. Only one strong reason would favor it—the call of God. This is where faith enters the picture and why it is a high point in this faith chapter. Real faith obeys God's call regardless of the stacked evidence on the other side. Such faith produces a prompt obedience in spite of all other factors involved: "By faith Abraham ... obeyed." This is the usual action for faith, but not always the one when a person thinks out his decision.

In 1936 a neighboring pastor, Arvid Ohrnell, resigned from his very fine church in Seattle. He said he felt a call to work full-time with the inmates of jails and prisons. Many of us who knew him recognized his sincerity but felt he faced an uncertain and difficult future. The depression was still on, he wasn't a member of a denomination, and he had no financial backers and the prisoners themselves were in no position to help. Some even questioned why a person would aspire to spend a lifetime with prisoners. Yet, like Abraham, he heard God's call, disdained the security of a more conventional ministry, and ventured forth not knowing what the future would bring. His faith was in God.

Arvid Ohrnell, a unique man, carved out for himself a unique ministry. Much of it was a restricted life of faith but it was interspersed with official positions that provided a semblance of normal security. He was a chaplain in a reformatory and prison representative for the Assemblies of God in the state of Washington and the nation. He was chaplain-at-large and pioneered a work that is now greatly expanded.

For over 30 years he talked, ate, slept, and breathed the work and welfare of his beloved prisoners. It was only fitting that when his end came it was in his sleep at the guest room behind the walls of a great southern penal institution.

Abraham hastily responded to God's call. He did not set up a prolonged time of mental wrestling or call a conference of his advisors. He didn't hesitate, stagger, or murmur because of the summons. He was ready, responsive, deliberate, and purposeful. He obeyed quickly. He had faith to sever old ties and to venture forth into the unknown. His goal was clear and he set his face like a flint to do God's bidding. He faced the unknown with no compass to direct him, no map to chart the way, and no guide to point the direction. He started at the prompting of God's voice and could only proceed by His enabling, guidance, and direction. Surely, this was an action of great faith. He heard God speak. He obeyed God's voice. He ventured at God's bidding. He leaned heavily on God each step of the way.

This great decision of Abraham involved renouncing certain things while embracing others. The contrast between what he gave up and what he received is most striking.

Possessions are items at hand that are tangible and real. Promises deal with the future and tend to be ethereal because the future is hazy and uncertain. Abraham had a good home. He gave it up for a promised one elsewhere. His cautious and practical neighbors must have looked askance at such a foolish venture and considered his action rash. If it had been in our day someone would have quoted the adage: "A bird in the hand is worth two in the bush."

If this chapter were a record of level-headed decisions Abraham would never have been cited as a model. Because it focuses on faith, however, he is one of the chief protagonists. The element of faith made an otherwise foolish venture a noble example. To this man of faith the promise of God was more durable than all his worldly possessions and his actions backed his belief.

Once again we are reminded that things are not what they seem to be. Our eyes tell us one thing while faith tells us another. Man says, "Seeing is believing," while God says, "Believing is seeing" (John 11:40). Those who have the insight of faith say with the apostle Paul: "We look not at the things which are seen, but at the things which are not seen: for the things which are seen are temporal; but the things which are not seen are eternal" (2 Corinthians 4:18).

When Abraham started on his long journey he was not counting on what his eyes could see as much as on a faith in the God who had called him. The invisible was more real to him than the visible. That is not a natural trait but very evidently one of faith—and his was a great faith.

Real faith stands the test of time. It endures many delays and does not get impatient. It waits for its reward and is confident it is coming. The time element is inconsequential.

To the ordinary man the present is of paramount importance while the future is secondary or completely ignored. To the man of faith the situation is reversed. Abraham is an example of one who puts the matter of time in right perspective. Only by faith in God's promise could this be done.

What a contrast there is between the city Abraham left and the one he sought. Ur was an ancient and well-established city. It was as permanent as anything men of that day could envision. The city Abraham sought by faith had been seen by no one. His compatriots could well have called it the figment of his own imagination. The situation is reversed today but the contrast is even greater. Where once stood the very beautiful city of Ur, there are now only shifting sand dunes hiding the evidence of an ancient civilization. The city that is now Abraham's habitation is vividly described for us by John:

> And the building of the wall of it was of jasper: and the city was pure gold, like unto clear glass. And the foundations of the wall of the city were garnished with all manner of precious stones. The first foundation was jasper; the second, sapphire; the third, a chalcedony; the fourth, an emerald; the fifth, sardonyx; the sixth, sardius; the seventh, chrysolite; the eighth, beryl; the ninth, a topaz; the tenth, a chrysoprasus; the eleventh, a jacinth; the twelfth, an amethyst. And the twelve gates were twelve pearls; every several gate was of one pearl: and the street of the city was pure gold, as it were transparent glass (Revelation 21:18-21).

By faith Abraham obeyed God. That faith enabled him to embrace the promises, see the invisible, plan for the future, discern between the passing and the permanent, and eventually inherit all God's provisions for His children.

7
Faith to Conceive

> Through faith also Sarah herself received strength to conceive seed, and was delivered of a child when she was past age, because she judged him faithful who had promised. Therefore sprang there even of one, and him as good as dead, so many as the stars of the sky in multitude, and as the sand which is by the seashore innumerable.
>
> Hebrews 11:11, 12

The exploits of faith cover many and varied aspects of life. Here it is extended to the conjugal bed and the mundane matter of conception and child bearing.

In this record the faith of Sarah is featured although it is interwoven with the exploits of her husband Abraham. A naturally reticent and retiring woman, Sarah believed God at a time and in such a way that it put her in the ranks of the illustrious exponents of faith. Few are the women who have reached this pinnacle, but she is one of whom all womankind can be justifiably proud. Although there were times in her life when faith was not particularly evident, in this instance she was a noble example to us all. Because of her faith great benefits came to her, her husband, and all posterity.

The faith of Sarah had to contend against some

very formidable obstacles. The possibility of her giving birth to a child was veritably nonexistent. She had been married for years and yet that union had produced no offspring. The very fact that Abraham had a son by Hagar was evidence that it was her barren condition that was at fault. Now she was over 90 years of age. If she could not conceive a child in her youth and middle years what possibility was there of her doing so when she was nearing the century mark? Common sense would classify such an event as impossible. Even the thought of it was contrary to experience as well as to nature.

If that weren't enough of a barrier there were the physical incapabilities of her husband Abraham. The years had taken their toll on him too. He was even older than Sarah. The record says he was "as good as dead." His potential for becoming a father was long gone. This was a time of life to be realistic and not be entertaining ideas of becoming parents. Could even faith face up to such a challenge?

But faith *did* surmount the obstacles. The faith of Sarah looked beyond the three menacing obstacles. She didn't consider the conditions, age, physical situation, facts of life, or the law of averages. She focused on the God who keeps His promises and changes not. God had spoken (Genesis 17:4, 16) and she was confident He would make good His word. With unwavering faith she laid hold on the physical vitality that made childbirth possible.

Although her husband was productively dead and she was long past the normal years of childbearing, she had faith to claim God's promise. By faith she embraced that son even before he was conceived. Wishful thinking, logical reasoning, willpower, or a concentrated thought life could not produce such a miracle. Only by faith could there be a restoration of the natural functions which had eroded with the years. Such was the faith of Sarah and by it she set a noble example for us.

The God of Abraham and Sarah still responds to the prayer of faith. Several times I heard Dr. Charles S. Price tell of an experience he had when praying for the sick. A young couple approached him. When asked which one needed prayer and what the affliction was they said neither one was ill. Then they confided in Dr. Price that they wanted a child but had been told it was impossible. They felt God could change that situation and wanted him to pray toward that end. He did pray and then dismissed the matter from his mind. About a year later a beaming couple, babe in arms, greeted the evangelist. It was the same couple and the baby had been born because of the prayer of faith.

That baby would be at least 50 years old now. I have often wondered who he or she is and if he/she is a person of great accomplishment or fame. This would be interesting to know but it is not vital to the story. The inescapable fact is that faith opened the barren womb in the past and does as much today.

If you ever conduct a Bible quiz I have a question to suggest. Ask your eager Bible students: "How many children did Abraham have?" The instinctive reply will be one—thinking of Isaac, the child of promise. On second thought some will answer two, as they remember Ishmael the son of Abraham and Hagar. The true answer is surprising. Abraham had eight children, one by Hagar, one by Sarah, and six by his second wife Keturah (25:2). When God does a job He does a good one! After Abraham had passed the century mark and was productively dead, the faith of his wife rejuvenated him so he could sire not only the son of promise but also six other sons after that.

Even though the faith of Sarah was outstanding, it in no way marked her as being perfect. None of the persons cited in this great gallery of faith was flawless. Evidence would indicate that a person can demonstrate great faith in one circumstance and fail to do so on other occasions. Because one shows great faith once is no indication that he is right or does so always. There is no greater demonstration of combined belief and unbelief than in the life of Sarah. Although her faith to conceive an heir while in her nineties was highly commendable, her reaction to God's promise at first was anything but exemplary.

Heavenly visitors initially visited the tent of Abraham and told him the good news. Sarah would become a mother and her progeny would constitute a great nation. In an adjacent tent, Sarah heard that remark. She reacted immediately, but not as expected from a matriarch or a woman of great faith. She guffawed and was highly amused at the preposterous idea. Perhaps it was not wholly a laugh of incredulity as she may not have known the message was from God. Her laughter was a cause of later embarrassment to her and she would rather have had it not known. Still, that initial reaction was anything but one of faith.

There is another example of an early lack of faith on the part of Sarah. God had promised Abraham a son and heir. Because she was his wife it would logically follow that the promise included her. Instead of taking that at face value she concocted a plan whereby her husband could have a son by her handmaid, Hagar (16:2). The idea was Sarah's and not Abraham's. It was as if her faith was not up to believing that God could fulfill His Word through her aging body.

Seeing the contrast of the weak and strong periods in Sarah's faith is helpful to us. It teaches us that faith is not always operative in the same strength even in the lives of these ancient celebrities. It reminds us that a person need not be perfect to exercise great faith. Even more encouraging is the fact that even we who have been filled with doubts and unbelief in the past can rise to great heights of faith.

Those who have casual acquaintance with these ancient Biblical records would view this incident as being rather minor. How would it qualify this woman to be listed in the great gallery of faith? A wife yearns for a baby and finally has one at a phenomenally old age. So what? That was nice for them and was something for their family to talk about. What more can it mean than that?

The faith of Sarah not only put a baby in her empty arms and brought delight to her home, it wielded a wide influence and profoundly changed the history of the world. As a result of that one supernatural birth a nation exists today that has rightly been called the miracle nation. The Jews have left their imprint on all the nations of the world throughout history and today have a restored homeland on which all the eyes of mankind are focused. Through the Jews came the Messiah and eventually the potent force of all Christendom. Who can measure its influence and power?

All of this came from the womb of a decrepit old woman who climaxed her life by taking God at His word. Who but God could do it in this way and who but one with exemplary faith in that great God could be a partner in the venture?

8
The Faith of a Pilgrim

These all died in faith, not having received the promises, but having seen them afar off, and were persuaded of them, and embraced them, and confessed that they were strangers and pilgrims on the earth. For they that say such things declare plainly that they seek a country.

And truly, if they had been mindful of that country from whence they came out, they might have had opportunity to have returned. But now they desire a better country, that is, a heavenly: wherefore God is not ashamed to be called their God: for he hath prepared for them a city.

Hebrews 11:13-16

The family of Abraham is renowned because of its faith. Not only is Abraham himself listed in this hall of fame, but his wife Sarah, his son Isaac, and his grandson Jacob are also there. Each one demonstrated his personal faith in God in a most unusual manner.

"These all died in faith." Could there be any more fitting epitaph than this? It speaks volumes. To be able to die in faith one must have lived in faith. The hopes and expectations they had throughout life remained strong as they passed through the portals of death. Although their grasp on material matters loosened, their hold on the promises remained firm.

While living, they counted the things to come as sure while what was at hand was uncertain. The promises of God were more real than present possessions. This is not the attitude or outlook of the natural man, but real faith in God makes it possible. It was just such a commendable faith that each of these persons had.

Two attitudes contributed to this great faith. One involved an unwavering confidence in God's promises. This is the aspect that we most generally stress and is vitally important. The other was their attitude toward the things of this life. The key to it is expressed in these words: "These all . . . confessed that they were strangers and pilgrims on the earth." Fully sensing that fact enabled them to look to God's promise for the future and to trust in His Word completely.

A pilgrim is a wanderer or wayfarer. He has no fixed abode or place of habitation. He is not a citizen of any one country nor does he have constitutional rights or privileges. In a more literal sense than we realize, Abraham and his family were nomads. They didn't put down their roots in any one place after receiving the call of God. The only land Abraham owned was the cave of Machpelah which was the family burial plot. In this way they could not, or did not, become attached to the things of this life that would come between them and God. Sensing in a real way that this world was not their home, they embraced God's promises and anticipated the home He was preparing for them.

The real Christian is also a pilgrim. Of course, not in the primitive sense of living in goat-skin tents and camping from place to place in the desert or renouncing his citizenship and responsibilities here on earth. The key is his attitude toward the things of this present life. His home here is less important than the one where he will spend eternity. Whether or not he has much of this world's goods is not as vital to him as having treasures in the secure vaults of heaven. If deprived of creature comforts here, it is not the calamity it would be if this were the only life he were to know. The Christian holds lightly the things of this life not because he doesn't enjoy them, but because eternal things are far more important. Having a real sense of values, he counts himself but a pilgrim here, sojourning temporarily, and enroute to eternal life in the city of God.

Ordinary reasoning cannot explain why any person would leave the comforts of normal life at home for the uncertainty of a nomadic life. Yet it has always happened, and still does, when individuals hear the clarion call of God.

No greater example of a modern vagabond can be cited than that of the intrepid Dutch woman, Corrie ten Boom. Hers has been a life of undaunted faith in spite of loneliness, dangers, imprisonment, and maltreatment. Now at a time when all those experiences are behind her she could well claim her few remaining days as time to live in ease and comfort. Instead she has done just the opposite. Although well in her eighties, she has chosen the rugged existence of an itinerant gospel worker in her self-styled role as "a tramp for the Lord." By faith she is spending the evening of her life bouncing from country to country and living out of a suitcase.

Abraham, Isaac, and Jacob exemplified the true faith of a pilgrim. We who would emulate them examine their lives that we might know the very principles of such faith and then demonstrate it as well. Just what, then, is pilgrim faith?

The faith of a pilgrim is focused on God. It does not look to circumstances or surroundings; therefore, it does not really matter if the situation is ideal or not. The hymn writer expressed it laconically: "My faith looks up to Thee." Faith always looks up and faith always looks to the Lord. When Peter looked to the Saviour he walked on the water, but when he looked at the waves he sank.

In an art gallery in London is a painting of a shepherd holding a lamb in his arms. Nearby is a wolf with bared fangs, leering at the innocent animal. The strong message of the picture lies in the gaze of the lamb. His eyes are not on the beast who would tear him limb from limb, but are looking confidently on the countenance of the shepherd.

The faith of a pilgrim is farsighted. The objects that are normally obscure and hazy loom up clearly to the person with such faith. It is as if his focus were set on that which is distant and blurs that which is close. He cannot be persuaded that such distant objects are unreal because he can see them so clearly.

An individual with such faith can expect to be criticized and misunderstood. Those with only normal vision will naturally assume that no one can see what they cannot. Such persons are quick to brand the man of faith as being visionary, impractical, and quixotic. He is dubbed as being so heavenly minded as to be of no earthly good. In spite of such accusations, the pilgrim plods on toward the distant city of God that is so real to him.

The faith of a pilgrim discerns between the temporal and the permanent. All too often we cling to objects of a temporary nature and overlook those of enduring qualities because we are confused as to which is which. We assume that the tangible is enduring and that the intangible is fleeting. The reverse is actually true. The apostle Paul speaks for all men of faith when he writes: "Meanwhile our eyes are fixed, not on the things that are seen, but on the things that are unseen: for what is seen passes away; what is unseen is eternal" (2 Corinthians 4:18, *NEB)*.

The one who lives as a pilgrim and has such faith knows which things are temporal and which are permanent. Such information is vitally important. It enables him to concentrate his energies and pursuits on what will count for both time and eternity. It makes possible his being a specialist in the area where it counts the most. What could be better than having such discernment?

The faith of a pilgrim is persistent and persevering. Such faith is not whimsical or capricious. It does not change with the weather, the tide, or human feelings. It lays hold on the promises of God and clings tenaciously to them. It exercises pertinacity far surpassing that of the most indomitable willpower. The faith of a pilgrim is one of inexhaustible patience.

George Mueller of Bristol, England is often cited as a modern apostle of faith. Many are the instances of speedy answers to his prayers. However, we often overlook some aspects of his faith. Early in his Christian life he started praying for the salvation of five men. Two of them were converted shortly after he started praying for them. Another was saved 40 years later. On his deathbed Mueller boldly asserted the others would be brought into the fold. One of them was saved at Mueller's funeral and the last one finally experienced God's grace 2 years later.

The faith of a pilgrim renounces the best the world has to offer. Pursuing God's best is not sufficient.

There must also be a renunciation of that which is essentially of this world. Abraham had an established home in Ur, one of the great cities of the ancient world. It was not discontentment that caused him to move, but rather the call of God. He renounced that wonderful place and continued to do so until his dying day.

In this citation of faith it says: "If they had wanted to they could have gone back to the good things of this world. But they didn't want to" (Hebrews 11:15, 16, *The Living Bible)*. Likewise, Moses renounced the wealth and pomp of one of the world's greatest nations to become a pilgrim leader of a pilgrim people (vv. 24-26). The pilgrim Christian turns his back on temporal things as he sets his face like a flint toward the eternal.

Abraham, the true pilgrim, is a type of and an example to every pilgrim Christian. He left one of the best earthly cities in pursuit of a heavenly one. In his day a city spoke of security. The ancient cities usually occupied a defensive hill site and had a water supply, walls, and gates, so they could withstand the onslaught of enemies from any side.

Cain sought to erect such a city in his pursuit of security (Genesis 4:17). He built one by his own ingenuity and labor, after having gone "out from the presence of the Lord" (v. 16). Only blowing sand remains at that ancient site today and the security he sought did not materialize. Abraham renounced an apparently strong fortress and lived as a pilgrim pursuing a city of God. The wisdom of his action is now evident to us. The erosion of time has long ago made Ur of the Chaldees extinct but the city of God endures for eternity.

No matter what security there may appear to be in this life, the pilgrim Christian holds it lightly. Happy is he who lives as a pilgrim and by faith counts more on the eternal city of God (Revelation 21:2-5) than anything in this world.

9
The Supreme Test

By faith Abraham, when he was tried, offered up Isaac: and he that had received the promises offered up his only begotten son, of whom it was said, That in Isaac shall thy seed be called: accounting that God was able to raise him up, even from the dead; from whence also he received him in a figure.

Hebrews 11:17-19

Abraham is a mighty giant of faith towering on the horizons of history. This incident marks his greatest triumph. Because of God's command, he passed through a treacherous valley of decision. He triumphed over a depth and intensity of anguish that would have swamped an ordinary person. Many of us wonder whether, under similar circumstances, we would have been equal to such an experience. No words can describe the pressures that he must have felt in making his decision of obedience. True faith is a tested faith. Great trials call for a great faith. This being the supreme test in the life of Abraham, faith reached its very apex in responding to it.

This outstanding episode of faith is predicated on two surprises. One is the shocking command of God and the other is the astounding response of Abraham to it. What kind of a God would demand a human sacrifice? What type of a father would accede to such a plan—and particularly if it involved his only son? Logic and common sense would count such action as unthinkable. Yet, it not only happened but is held up to us as exemplary conduct.

The fact that the whole experience worked out for the glory of God and the good of Abraham is in itself a tribute to the basic ingredient of faith that made such a result possible. It is an Old Testament event that demonstrates a New Testament principle: "And we know that all things work together for good to them that love God, to them who are the called according to his purpose" (Romans 8:28). All ingredients that go into a doctor's prescription are not good. Some are actually poison. The combination, however, produces a good effect to combat the illness of the patient. All of the ingredients in the crucible of life are not good, but under the wise direction of God they *work together* for good when mixed with faith.

Have you ever, in time of deep depression, seriously questioned God or His Word? While battling insidious doubts and blasphemous misgivings have you been tempted to give up in despair? Have apparent contradictions loomed up like mountains and encircled you? Does God contradict himself or does it only appear to be so to the troubled soul? If this has been your experience then you can easily identify with Abraham.

An ordinary person in the position of Abraham would find it impossible to reason his way through the morass of apparent contradictions. God had promised him innumerable descendants (Genesis 15:5). He was assured that this would come to pass through Isaac (21:12,18). Now the same God said:

"Take . . . thine only son Isaac . . . and offer him . . . for a burnt offering" (22:2).

Surely this wasn't right. It was contrary to basic morality, and particularly to kill an innocent party. It was revolting to natural feelings and affections. Why would that be pleasing to God? It was a glaring contradiction to what He had previously said. Had God changed His mind and, if so, why? The magnitude of the problem is described by Matthew Henry:

> After he had received the promise that his Isaac should build up his family, and that "in him his seed should be called" (Hebrews 11:18), and that he should be one of the progenitors of the Messiah, and all nations blessed in Him; so that in being called to offer up his Isaac, he seemed to be called to destroy and cut off his own family, to cancel the promises of God, to prevent the coming of Christ, to destroy the whole truth, to sacrifice his own soul and his hope of salvation, to cut off the church of God at one blow; a most terrible trial.

Then, out of the maze of human reasoning, apparent contradictions, and forebodings of calamity, faith came striding to the fore. It took command of the situation and everything changed. Faith got a grip on God and after that nothing else mattered. The faith of Abraham looked beyond the contradictions as if they did not exist. He obeyed God's command. The situation changed from defeat to victory. A similar faith in the same God can do the same for you.

What prompted God to call for this severe trial? Why would He want to do anything that would have even the slightest tendency to make Him look inconsistent? Certainly it was not a selfish motive on His part. Neither did it have anything to do with Isaac, although it involved him so vitally. The whole plan was instituted for the good of Abraham and the strengthening of his faith. God did not want the life of Isaac but the will of Abraham. He saw the benefits that would accrue to Abraham and how he would come through the trial triumphantly. With that ultimate end in view he called for Isaac to be offered as a sacrifice. Although it is often hard for us to comprehend, the divine principle is true: "The trial of your faith [is] much more precious than . . . gold" (1 Peter 1:7).

How easy it is to lapse from the posture of faith. We tend to see the means involved and somewhat lose sight of the God who is responsible for the action. Rather insidiously those means become an idol and must eventually be destroyed as was the brazen serpent (2 Kings 18:4). When God's answer comes we are prone to suppose that faith is not quite as essential as it was before. It could be that this is what happened to Abraham.

When God promised him a son the very thought seemed preposterous. Every circumstance seemed to indicate it couldn't happen. Faith clung to the promise, however, and it did come to pass. After Isaac was born it became easy to dote on the baby instead of the God who made his birth possible. Then for 17 years he pinned his hopes on that great son of his. Isaac was the pride of his life and all his expectations centered in him. Could it be that after having an initial faith in God his gaze had shifted to Isaac?

Then the supreme test came: The God who made Isaac's birth possible commanded he must die. Not only must Abraham consent to it but he must witness the death and, horror of horrors, be the executioner. Could anything be more severe than this? If he carried out that plan, all his earthly hopes would be dashed and he would be the object of reproach and ridicule. Thank God, Abraham met the test gloriously. His faith was not in Isaac but in God. Even if Isaac died he could stand on God's original promise. Faith held out for the miraculous and told him that God was able to raise Isaac up, even from the dead. What a gigantic faith in an omnipotent God!

The decision of Abraham was a speedy and lonely one. There was no prolonged wringing of the hands, sobs, or tears. Evidence points to the fact that he made his decision before retiring which enabled him to have a good night's sleep. Then he was up early to start the journey. Nothing on record indicates he consulted with anyone; not even Isaac was taken into his confidence. None of his peers made the 2-day trip with him—only two servant lads who took orders and stood afar off. Many of us would reach out for all the numerical support obtainable in such an ordeal. Abraham did just the opposite. He knew that good, influential friends or relatives would have tried to talk him out of such a rash act. He knew what others have learned the hard way: the choice of faith is a lonely one. Great decisions of faith do not come out of a committee or a conference session. They are made by one man standing on the bleak peak of leadership. Such a man was Abraham and such a decision was his.

Faith is not only conspicuous in the daring decision and determined action of Abraham but in his words as well. It so saturated his whole being that it veritably oozed out of every pore. In reply to his son's inquiry about an animal for the sacrifice, he spoke what is a cornerstone of God's great plan of redemption. He said: "My son, God will provide . . . a lamb." Not only was this a prediction of what would happen on Mount Moriah but it would be true in a greater sense on Mount Calvary. Only by faith could he have such an insight and perceive such a happening.

Even in addressing the servants he gave an indication of what would definitely transpire: "And Abraham said unto his young men, Abide ye here with the ass; and I and the lad will go yonder and worship, *and come again* to you." He did not expect to walk down that slope alone. He had every confidence that Isaac would be with him. Knowing what he intended to do, it was only faith that could bring him to that conclusion.

A faithful missionary couple labored in a very difficult field. For over 20 years they preached and witnessed but didn't see even one convert.

A missionary group in the homeland wanted to send them something and wrote asking if they had a particular need. In reply they requested a Communion set. Just as Abraham was sure that he and the lad would come down again, so they were confident there would be converts and they wanted the Communion set available when it happened. Such faith will surely see its reward.

Is the Hebrews account of this event accurate? It says: "By faith Abraham . . . offered up Isaac." An ordinary eyewitness would have answered in the negative. A newspaper reporter would have told another story. Here, again, is evidence that God sees factors beyond our knowledge. He saw Abraham's willingness to make the sacrifice and counted it for the deed. In that sense, the record is exceedingly accurate. When Abraham lifted the dagger the sacrifice was complete.

Behind his willingness to slay his son was an unshakable confidence in God. He had no doubt but what God could, and would, raise Isaac from the dead. That would have been a miracle, but no greater a one than Isaac's birth. In the miracle of Isaac's birth God had provided a power that was lacking in nature. Had he been slain on the altar God would only have had to restore life that had been taken away at His command. Faith conveyed to Abraham that even a resurrection was easy for God in demonstrating that He consistently keeps all His promises.

One remarkable aspect of this whole episode was Isaac's attitude. Evidently he did not know to what extent he was to be involved in the matter. Somewhere along the line, however, he must have become aware that his life was in jeopardy. Surely it must have been evident to him when the two stood by the altar and his father began to bind him with a rope. The natural action would have been to rebel. His father was old and gnarled while he was vigorous and strong. Isaac could have wrestled free and run down the slope, appealing to the servants to keep him from the grasp of one who had suddenly lost his sense of reason. Instead, he was totally submissive. He must have been a willing sacrifice, and that speaks either of his own great faith or at least of his complete confidence in his father. Whichever it was, it speaks well for Isaac and he deserves credit also, even though the towering faith is that of Abraham.

Not to be overlooked is the fact that the events of Genesis 22 provide a unique telescopic glimpse into the future. What happened on Mount Moriah prefigured what would transpire 2,000 years later on Mount Calvary. These two important locations are almost on the same geographical spot. The general area of Moriah included what was later called Calvary.

In both places a father offered a son in sacrifice.

Both sons were willing and submissive in spite of the extreme cost to them. In both instances God provided the lamb. It could be said of Abraham as well as Jehovah: "He . . . spared not his own Son"(Romans 8:32). It was equally true of Isaac as it was of Jesus: "He . . . became obedient unto death" (Philippians 2:8). Jesus was dead for 3 days. In the mind of Abraham Isaac was dead for the same period of time, between his decision and God's intervention. Abraham counted a resurrection as possible and God demonstrated it in raising up Jesus. A substitute died in the place of Isaac on Mount Moriah and he could walk away a free man. A Substitute died for us on Mount Calvary and we are free because of it.

The supreme test of the faith of Abraham not only worked for his good, but also, by example, for the good of all who will follow in his footsteps.

10
Deathbed Testimonies

> By faith Isaac blessed Jacob and Esau concerning things to come. By faith Jacob, when he was a dying, blessed both the sons of Joseph . . ., leaning upon . . . his staff.
>
> Hebrews 11:20, 21

Natural vision and insight are very limited when one is on his deathbed. As death approaches, time and circumstances tend to close in and restrict interest to the events of the moment. When the added element of faith is injected, however, the whole situation is changed. New vistas appear on an expanded horizon and the picture is entirely different.

The next three verses in this great faith chapter are brief references to deathbed pronouncements by patriarchs of old. The first two involve the blessings the men imparted to their progeny and the other one deals with the disposal of a patriarch's own body. Because of the similarity, we shall deal with the first two together and the other one just a bit later.

Although both Isaac and Jacob lived long and colorful lives, their examples of faith came out of their waning moments. Isaac lived longer than any of the four great patriarchs, yet only a brief sentence pinpoints his faith (Hebrews 11:20). This terse statement alludes to the details recorded in Genesis 27. What appears to be somewhat incidental and commonplace is actually a high point when viewed in the category of exploits of faith.

The outstanding factor in the faith of Isaac is that he pronounced a benediction upon Jacob and declared what would happen to him in the future. Nothing else is mentioned in this citation. The family maneuverings leading up to that transaction are puzzling to us and tend to sidetrack us from the main issue. Both parents were guilty of partiality and used chicanery and trickery to get God's unique blessing for his or her favorite son. The tactics used were despicable as well as futile and unnecessary.

In spite of such knavery, God has His way of bringing about His will and plan. Isaac schemed to trick God into blessing his favorite, Esau, but another trick disrupted his plan and eventually God's will was done. Rebekah knew that the younger of the twins would be the dominant leader, as God had imparted that knowledge to her before their birth (Genesis 25:23). It is hard to conceive that she had not passed on that information to her husband. It is not important that paternal partiality initiated one plan and failed. Neither is it significant as to whether it was originally the plan of the mother or father. In the final action, a man comprehended by faith what was God's plan for his sons and his words proclaimed that plan. Faith embraces and declares that which is God's will.

It is significant that Isaac blessed both his sons. Those parental blessings dovetailed with the plan of God for each man. He did not say the same words or predict the same results. By faith he envisioned what would transpire in each individual life and his words were later verified.

Using colorful words and descriptive phrases Isaac spelled out what was ahead for each son. To Jacob he said: "Therefore God give thee of the dew of heaven, and the fatness of the earth, and plenty of corn and wine: let people serve thee, and nations bow down to thee: be lord over thy brethren, and let thy mother's sons bow down to thee: cursed be every one that curseth thee, and blessed be he that blesseth thee" (27:28, 29). To Esau he said: "Behold, thy dwelling shall be the fatness of the earth, and of the dew of heaven from above; and by thy sword shalt thou live, and shalt serve thy brother: and it shall come to pass when thou shalt have the dominion, that thou shalt break his yoke from off thy neck" (vv. 39, 40).

Each son received a blessing and a role that, in God's wisdom, was suitable to his nature, talents, and capacity. By faith Isaac sensed all this and had a part in declaring it while it was yet in the future. Faith looks to the future even if the man himself has no future. His physical eyes were dim but his spiritual discernment was not. The faith of Isaac overcame even his natural partiality to Esau and caused him to give the principal blessing to Jacob. He recognized and acquiesced to God's plan although his original preference ran counter to it. True faith reckons on God and acknowledges that His plan will be enacted whatever the varying circumstances or actions of men. "[With eyes of] faith Isaac, looking far into the future, invoked blessings upon Jacob and Esau" *(Amplified)*.

It is strikingly interesting that the faith of both father and son should be so similar and be recorded in tandem in this great faith chapter of the Bible.

How often there are scenes reenacted from generation to generation. In the lives of both Isaac and Jacob there is but one highlight of faith listed and each came as death neared. In each case it involved blessing his progeny. Jacob's action consisted of giving the patriarchal blessing to his grandsons, Ephraim and Manasseh. They had been born to Joseph and his Egyptian wife in a foreign land. By Jacob's act of faith they were being assured that there would be no discrimination against them and that they were indeed to be recipients of the full blessings of the covenant (Genesis 48:5, 16, 20).

The period just before death is a good testing ground for faith. If there is to be a time in life when faith is at a low ebb it is best that it be any other time than when one approaches that dark valley. It must be conceded that Jacob was not always a man of faith, but when it really counted, he was. In both his life and that of his father, faith was at its high point just before their departure from this life.

Deathbed faith is in no way inferior faith. It was not so in the lives of Isaac, Jacob, and Joseph. Another classic example of such faith is that of the thief on the cross.

The faith of that dying criminal had to contend with circumstances that would have staggered an ordinary faith. He believed while he saw Christ dying the death of a felon. He believed when the disciples were anything but examples of loyalty. He believed while suffering torture and pain. He believed while surrounded by scoffers and skeptics. Who could discredit such a faith?

In the act of blessing his grandsons Jacob glanced back over his past life and forward into their lives to come. He was acutely conscious of God having led and blessed him and was positive Jehovah would do the same for his posterity. Five times God had appeared to Jacob and each time it involved correcting his ways. He boldly declared that with such guidance Ephraim and Manasseh would also walk in the path of blessing. He said: "The angel which redeemed me from all evil, bless the lads; and let my name be named on them and the name of my fathers Abraham and Isaac" (v. 16).

By faith Jacob had an insight into the plan of God for each of the young men. That faith defied custom and tradition and bestowed the principal blessing on the younger son. In so doing, Jacob recognized the sovereignty of God that permits Him to do as He sees fit. Faith not only recognizes God's plan but adjusts to it. He put the last one first and the first one last. When Jacob crossed his hands he emblematically foreshadowed the cross by which outcasts become the recipients of God's blessing even before the chosen ones (Matthew 21:31).

Another facet of Jacob's faith (although not mentioned in Hebrews) was his firm conviction that his family would be returned to the land of promise where he had previously lived. The promise had been reiterated in each generation and his faith counted it as a fact. When he had qualms about leaving Canaan, God had assured him the family would return (Genesis 46:4). Now when he was dying he was still confident it would come to pass (48:21). Although circumstances seemed to indicate otherwise, faith declared it would happen.

A question has often been raised as to what bearing the staff had in this matter and why it should even be mentioned in such a brief statement about Jacob's faith. There are three possible meanings and it could be that all three are true. It is very likely he leaned on his staff because of his physical frailty. He was in bed at the time. Mustering what limited strength he had, he pulled himself upright for the special occasion. With great authority he pronounced the blessing while being supported by the staff. By that he was saying that although he was failing, God's promise was still true.

Also, the staff was an ensign of his office as the patriarchal head of a large family. In that way it must be a part of the blessing ritual and the act of worship. A third aspect is that there is symbolic significance to his leaning on the staff. In the past he had mentioned the staff when acknowledging his utter dependence on God (32:10). The prominence of his staff in this transaction would indicate the same.

It is highly significant that at the end of his life Jacob was using his limited energies to worship God. True faith leads to worship. It envisions a great God as contrasted with man's frailty. It brings to man a sense of his indebtedness and a desire to worship the God who made him and sustains his life.

11
The Preaching Mummy

By faith Joseph, when he died, made mention of the departing of the children of Israel; and gave commandment concerning his bones.

Hebrews 11:22

The examples cited in this great gallery of faith are often surprising and startling. None is more extraordinary than this obscure incident recorded from the life of Joseph. His biography is long, packed with noble activities, teeming with traces of God's leading, and abounding with evidences of faith. Yet, all these incidents are bypassed to concentrate on a twofold utterance he spoke on his deathbed.

The casual reader is apt to assume that a weak example of faith is used when many strong ones are available. A further probing, however, will prove this to be one of the greatest specimens of faith in the life of Joseph. It further attests to the fact that what we often judge as being of little significance God counts as vitally important.

Let us transport ourselves back across the ages to the deathbed of Joseph. Often a person's final words have particular weight and significance. From our vantage point we know that is true of Joseph's dying words because they have stood through the centuries as an example of fervid faith. His deep involvement in God's plan for Israel was still strong at the gates of death and he was determined it should be afterward.

There are two facets to the faith-inspired deathbed utterance of Joseph. The most important one comes first and then the intriguing and unusual one follows. He confidently reminded his children that the Israelites would eventually leave the land in which they were then prospering and gave specific instructions about the disposition of his body at that time: "It was by faith that Joseph on his deathbed spoke of the exodus of the Israelites, and gave confident orders about the disposal of his own mortal remains" *(Phillips)*.

Logical reasoning and faith do not always come up with the same answer. Had Joseph merely reasoned things out his advice would likely have been different. He had lived all of his adult life in Egypt. Despite a time of imprisonment on false charges, he eventually came to a place of prominent leadership beyond his most visionary expectations. He was the prime minister of all Egypt and second only to the king. Because of his position he had been able to help his father and his brothers, and the Israelites were greatly favored because of their relationship to Joseph.

At the time of his death Joseph was at the summit of his prosperity, as were his children and his people. Common logic would have said, "You've never had it so good. Stay where you are no matter what happens." On the other hand, it was faith that reminded them there was coming a time when they would return to their former home.

Joseph considered something else besides the prosperity and prominence of the Israelites in Egypt. Two hundred years before God had made a covenant with his great grandfather, Abraham, and Joseph still remembered it: "And he said unto Abram, Know of a surety that thy seed shall be a stranger in a land that is not theirs, and shall serve them; and they shall afflict them four hundred years. . . . But in the fourth generation they shall come hither again" (Genesis 15:13, 16).

There were no natural indications that another king would arise "who knew not Joseph," or that a favored people would become oppressed slaves, or that they would even desire to go back to the land where their forebears had almost starved in times of famine. Yet, God had declared that these surprising events would transpire. Natural circumstances and common reasoning dictated one course of action, while God's spoken word pointed to another.

Note carefully what Joseph could have easily said but didn't. He didn't say: "I have worked hard to give you advantages. Now don't give up all these benefits just on a whimsical idea that there are greener pastures elsewhere." He didn't say: "Forget the idea that things will get worse. That's only pessimism." He didn't say: "There are better days ahead and you can't go anywhere but up."

He didn't even do what it would have been easiest to do—forget all about what God had predicted to Abraham. Instead, he hinged his own forecast for their future on God's ancient utterance: "By *faith* Joseph . . . made mention of the departing of the children of Israel." Faith takes God at His word and counts on it even when it contradicts all other evidences. Faith is farsighted and looks beyond current conditions and circumstances. That was the kind of faith that Joseph exhibited.

The faith of Joseph was vastly different from even

the faith that is usually commended. It had to contend against severely difficult obstacles and did so without staggering. Most faith surveys the debris of disappointment, discouragement, financial reverses, sickness, suffering, and bereavement, and says: "Things are bad but I believe God that they will get better." Joseph veritably said: "Things are going good for all of us but I believe God's word and know it is going to get much worse." Even an optimist without faith can cheerfully make the first statement. It takes a double portion of faith to believe God for future events that you don't relish or desire. That was the remarkable faith Joseph evidenced by his dying words.

Now we must consider the second phase of Joseph's deathbed statement which had to do with the interment of his body. It is not uncommon for a person to give instructions for the disposal of his earthly remains. Then why should this be so important in this matter of faith? Is it even related to faith, much less an example so outstanding as to be recorded in the annals of great exploits?

Three references in the Old Testament tell the whole story about the burial instructions and the prolonged process of burying Joseph. One gives his request for a deferred interment, the second tells about Moses taking the body from Egypt over 300 years later, and the third relates the account of the burial in Schechem 60 years after that:

> And Joseph took an oath of the children of Israel, saying, God will surely visit you, and ye shall carry up my bones from hence (Genesis 50:25).
>
> And Moses took the bones of Joseph with him: for he had straitly sworn the children of Israel, saying, God

will surely visit you; and ye shall carry up my bones away hence with you (Exodus 13:19).

And the bones of Joseph, which the children of Israel brought up out of Egypt, buried they in Schechem, in a parcel of ground which Jacob bought of the sons of Hamor the father of Schechem for a hundred pieces of silver; and it became the inheritance of the children of Joseph (Joshua 24:32).

Joseph's request was much more than that he be buried in the family plot in the land of Canaan. The intervening time between his death and eventual burial made it strikingly different. His own father, Jacob, had requested to be buried in his homeland and the family had made a pilgrimage to perform that sad task. This too could have been done for Joseph but those weren't his instructions. He purposely planned for a long delay between his death and burial. It was there that faith was exercised and demonstrated.

The last verse of Genesis puts the capstone on the biography of Joseph and hints at a very strange procedure: "So Joseph died, being a hundred and ten years old: and they embalmed him, and he was put in a coffin in Egypt." There is an inference here that is most interesting. Instead of being entombed in the usual manner, the body of Joseph was embalmed and placed in a stone sarcophagus and very likely exposed to view in the open air or in a public place. It would seem evident that his instructions were that he not be buried at all in Egypt but interment should wait until his posterity got back permanently to the land of promise. The formal story of his life ended with him "in a coffin in Egypt."

How does this request and action exemplify faith? As the prime minister of Egypt he could have been highly honored by being buried in a pyramid. As a loyal son of Abraham, Isaac, and Jacob he could have requested burial beside one of them. As one with means he could have chosen a picturesque site for his interment. He asked not that his history be chiseled on an obelisk or on the temple facade or etched on papyrus.

Instead, he requested that he not be buried at all—until God's promise was fulfilled. He was willing to risk not being buried if God's promise would not come to pass. He chose deferred burial to highlight the faithfulness of God to keep His word. But what if his posterity never left Egypt? Then reproach would be his always. He lost sight of that, however, in a faith that laid hold on what God had spoken, and he was confident it would happen. This was a spectacular act of faith. It embodied not only words but demonstrable action as well.

There was even a stronger reason for the body of Joseph not being buried. Following the ancient Egyptian art, his body was embalmed and put on display according to his request. The sight of that coffin containing the remains of Joseph was a constant reminder to every passerby. As a young man he believed God, in prison his faith did not waver, in the affluence and influence of leadership he remained true to Jehovah, when on his deathbed he reminded his children of God's promise, and in an embalmed state he continued to proclaim that truth.

That mummy, in a conspicuous place, preached God's truth long after Joseph himself had expired. When those of another generation would ask about their illustrious ancestor and wonder at his not being properly buried, they would be reminded of what God had said and what Joseph so firmly believed would happen. Joseph lived only 110 years but his unburied body was a witness for three times that long to his faith and God's faithfulness.

During the prosperous years for the Israelites in Egypt the body of Joseph proclaimed, "Things will get worse." In later times of adversity, oppressive slavery, and tyrannical misery it declared, "Things will get better." Circumstances may change but God's declarations remain ever the same—and will surely come to pass. This is the faith of godly Joseph. This is the message of the preaching mummy.

12
Parental Faith

> By faith Moses, when he was born, was hid three months of his parents, because they saw he was a proper child; and they were not afraid of the king's commandment.
>
> Hebrews 1:23

Real faith does not always catapult a person into the limelight or make his name a household word. No better example of that fact can be found than in this very incident. At first glance this verse seems to pertain to the faith of Moses. Yet, upon closer scrutiny, it is evident that it refers to the faith of two people whose names are not even mentioned. Who, except students of genealogies, would know who Amram and Jochebed were? Theirs was a faith worthy of being cited in this great gallery of faith and yet their names were omitted. Their introduction into this record hinges upon the name of their famous son, Moses.

The faith of Moses' parents was far more productive and important than it would appear on the surface. They exercised great faith in God, on behalf of their son, long before he was even aware of what was going on. Although history pays tribute to the eminent emancipator of Israel and to the faith that made him such a leader, it tends to overlook what happened before that. If it hadn't been for the faith of Amram and Jochebed there would never have been a Moses. How often the faithfulness of inconspicuous persons makes possible a life and ministry that influences multitudes.

The details of how the baby Moses was spared are undeniably fascinating. Far more intriguing is the symbolic meaning behind those events. What happened when that Hebrew babe was delivered from death is a type of how salvation and life has come to all mankind.

By decree of the king, Moses was destined to die. All male Hebrew babies were to be thrown into the river and drowned (Exodus 1:22). When Moses was 3 months old an inspection was to be made of all Hebrew homes and it was necessary that a new hiding place be found. His mother actually put him in the river. She made a little boat of papyrus reeds and waterproofed it with pitch. Instead of drowning he was able to live—all because of that little pitch-covered vessel.

The full impact of this action strikes us when we realize that the word *pitch* stems from the same root word as *atonement.* Pitch made the difference between Moses' living and dying. The atonement provided by our Saviour makes the difference between our succumbing to sin and death and triumphing over them.

By faith Noah built an ark and escaped the judgment by water that came upon the earth. The parents of Moses did a similar thing but on a smaller scale. By faith they built an ark so their son might escape the massacre of a wicked king and thus be spared to become the emancipator of his people. Through the atonement of Christ an ark of safety is provided so we can escape the judgment to come upon the world and live eternally.

This outstanding feat of faith was a joint venture of a husband and wife. In the most detailed account of the plan the wife, Jochebed, is given prominence (Exodus 2:2, 3). Amram, the husband, is alluded to in Stephen's sermon (Acts 7:20), and here in this citation the faith is attributed to both of them. Without a doubt both parents were involved in the decision. They shared an unshakable belief in God and a sublime parental confidence that their son was destined for heights of greatness in God that were worthy of any risk involved. They sensed there was something unusual about the son who was given to them.

In the plethora of modern translations of the Scriptures we have a variety of descriptions of the child: "a fine child," "an exceptional child," "fair," "unusual," "handsome," "proper," "goodly," "comely," and "the rare loveliness of the child." In spite of all these descriptions, however, we are reminded that their faith, not his beauty or other attributes, caused them to spare his life at the risk of their own. There was just something about the child that caused them to believe God on his behalf.

How blessed it is when parents stand together in radiant, productive faith. Their faith contributes much to the life and well-being of their offspring. As in this instance, it often makes possible an outstanding faith in their children.

A basic characteristic of faith is that it always points toward, and integrates into, the purpose and plan of God. Whether or not it does so is a test of its true quality. A person exercising such faith moves with God although it may cause him to be out of step with others. Such was the unusual faith of these Hebrew parents.

In this instance, there was a sharp conflict between Pharaoh's plan for the Children of Israel and what God purposed for them. The proclamation to kill all male babies was calculated to rob the Hebrews of leadership and keep them in subjection. It struck at the very foundation of what Jehovah had promised Abraham, Isaac, and Jacob. Pharaoh envisioned them as slaves for generations to come and took steps to make that possible. God saw them as a free people living in the land of promise.

The faith of these godly parents embraced God's plan even though it meant defying the fearful edict of their king. When God's plan and men's schemes are at cross-purposes, faith senses the move of God and steps forth boldly to walk in that way. The stalwart faith of Amram and Jochebed defied the command of a mighty potentate and they are lauded for their fearless action. In the later era of the Apostolic Church, Peter did likewise and summed up the matter succinctly: "We ought to obey God rather than men" (Acts 5:29).

The choice of faith may or may not flow in the same channel as our natural affections. God is not limited to do just what we desire nor is He confined to the boundaries of our normal tendencies. The Bible gives examples where God's workings followed the stream of human love and also where they went contrary to it. In this case, the instinctive yearning of the parents to save their son coincided perfectly with God's plan. An example of the opposite is found in the life of Abraham. He was commanded by God to slay his beloved son as a sacrifice to Jehovah. Although it was intended only as a test, his faith responded to it. Even the thought of such a deed was repulsive to him, but because of his great faith in God he followed the instructions.

Faith understands that God's voice and plan takes supremacy over the commands of men, human reasoning, filial love, and the dictates of circumstances. He who has such faith will predicate his actions on its promptings whether or not it is consistent with these other dominant forces. The inferior authority must always give way to the superior.

The faith of parents can profoundly affect the lives of their offspring. Although they cannot present to them a prepackaged salvation, they can give them a heritage and background of faith. Such a legacy gives children a running start in this race where faith is so vital.

My father was a businessman and a devout Christian. He died before reaching 50, while I was but 6 years old. The work of the gospel was dear to his heart. He would have been the happiest person alive if the call of God to preach had been entrusted to him.

The Sunday after his funeral my mother, with her two small sons, attended the house of God as they usually did. That morning the pastor preached from dual texts: "Thus saith the Lord, Thou shalt not build me a house to dwell in" (1 Chronicles 17:4). "And it shall come to pass, when thy days be expired . . . that I will raise up thy seed after thee, which shall be of thy sons . . . . He shall build me a house" (vv. 11, 12). David was only permitted to gather the materials, but his son Solomon erected the temple that he so aspired to build.

The truth of that sermon was timely and comforting to the young widow. Only after I had been in the ministry many years did she relate this incident to me. Her faith had laid claim to that role for me to carry out what my father had so wanted to do. He had assembled a Bible reference library which I was destined to inherit and it has been an integral part of my life and ministry.

That is only a minor way in which he assembled materials I have been able to use in building for eternity. Only the records of heaven will reveal the input of both my parents into my ministry. Only recently I stood at the grave of my father and hoped he was aware that his son has preached the gospel almost as long as he lived.

The faith of Abraham and Sarah made it possible for Isaac to be born. The faith of Amram and Jochebed brought about the sparing of Moses after he was born. The faith of Noah provided an escape for his family from the judgmental deluge. Who, but God, can trace the chain of events stemming from parents who demonstrate unwavering faith?

13
The Process of Making a Decision

By faith Moses, when he was come to years, refused to be called the son of Pharaoh's daughter; choosing rather to suffer affliction with the people of God, than to enjoy the pleasures of sin for a season; esteeming the reproach of Christ greater riches than the treasures of Egypt: for he had respect unto the recompence of the reward.

By faith he forsook Egypt, not fearing the wrath of the king: for he endured, as seeing him who is invisible.

Hebrews 11:24-27

Making decisions is a necessary part of living. Whether we like it or not life confronts each of us with demands for course-changing decisions that determine our individual destiny. An astronaut hurtling through space changes his course and pinpoints his target by firing a rocket engine a specified number of seconds. In much the same way, each choice we make contributes something toward our ultimate goal.

Moses made a momentous decision that not only had a drastic effect on his own life but also on the nation of Israel and the history of the world. It was not in any sense an easy one. Few individuals in his shoes would have chosen the course he took. It is of vital interest to us to know just how he arrived at that choice.

First, faith was at the very heart of his resolute decision. Although Moses had proven maturity, rare discretion, objective judgment, and a sensitive conscience, it was a great faith in God that enabled him to take the action he did. Such a faith brought God into his reckoning and that was the greatest factor in his weighty decision. We are able to learn much from the process by which he came to his conclusion.

A person must refuse before he can choose. Refusing and choosing are linked together and are invariably in that order. One is the negative aspect of the choice and the other is the positive. One is the act of relinquishment and the other that of embracing. The individual must turn his back on old affairs if he is to pursue that which is right and new.

The renunciation of Moses involved a way of life to which he had been accustomed as long as he could remember. It was a life of opulence with all the "creature comforts" of the royal family. He gave up the perquisites and privileges of the king's grandson to cast his lot with a nomadic slave people. He was well aware that his being a resident of the royal palace would preclude his being able to help the Israelites. Until he renounced his former life he was sanctioning the policy of repression against the people of God. In that way his renunciation was a necessary first step in his decision of faith.

Jesus emphasized the primacy of renunciation when He said: "If any man will come after me, let him *deny himself*, and take up his cross, and follow me" (Matthew 16:24). The denial of self is shown by the refusal of Moses. The great act of faith that brings eternal life starts with denying self and ends up in following Jesus.

The choice of Moses was a weighty one. Making a decision often calls for more strength than carrying it out. His choice was not thrust upon him or forced by outside pressures. He demonstrated no reluctance at all. Of his own volition he made a decision that determined his destiny.

Choosing is the positive aspect of making a decision. It involves aggressive, vigorous action. It goes far beyond knowing what should be done, talking about it, or even wrestling with the problem. Very often making such a choice involves a tremendous sacrifice. It was true in this instance. The Jewish historian Josephus says Moses was destined for the throne of Egypt. Yet with calculated determination that is puzzling to the average person, he chose a far more lowly path.

What elements went into making this decision? Was it the result of logical reasoning? Was it merely that Moses was one of those strange persons with a natural distaste for the affluent life of a palace? Was it only the strong pull of blood ties or nationality? Each of these forces might influence others but it is clearly evident none of them was the basis of his choice. Natural logic would have led him to believe he could really help the slaves if he were granted time and eventually became king. Ordinary thinking would say that was the plausible way to help them.

Ruling out these and other points of logic, he exercised faith and made the greatest choice of his life. By faith he embraced the promise and plan of God. It was not only God's plan that the Israelites be free but also that they live in the promised land. By faith Moses believed that promise (Genesis 46:4) and sensed that the time for the fulfillment of God's plan was at hand. Motivated by faith, he counted it his greatest service to submit his life to the will and purpose of God. Faith told him all other matters were of less importance than the path he chose to pursue. What a choice! What a decision!

In this momentous decision Moses exercised an uncanny sense of true values. His friends at the time would judge that he had made a poor bargain. He forsook a life that many would aspire to and took on reproach, a gigantic task, the headaches of leadership, and a nomadic, uncertain existence. Instead of faulty calculations, however, his perception was sharp and his acumen most penetrative.

Others would judge his actions without having the insight to all the facts that were at his disposal. What he saw that others did not see was enough to tip the scale. He knew his decision was right and time has proven it to be one of the greatest decisions of history.

It was not innate ability but faith that gave Moses that valuable insight. What he saw beyond the veil of natural perception far surpassed what he could claim for the present. The Weymouth translation says: "He fixed his gaze upon the coming reward." When he surveyed the whole situation and appraised the assets and the liabilities, he made the choice that was to be the best for him and his people. Without faith he would have been nearsighted and would likely have chosen the life of a mere grandson of the king instead of being one of God's noblemen.

As with Moses, faith also counterbalances our limited natural reasoning and makes it possible for us to make decisions with eternal values in view. The man of faith steps forth with confidence because his appraisals are reckoned on God and a sense of His will. Because of his faith, he knows what is really important. His decisions are often predicated on what others do not see or perceive. What appears to be a foolish move to others proves to be a wise one indeed. If faith is a part of your calculations it will change your viewpoints and your conclusions.

By faith Moses was able to abandon Egypt completely. He was confident of each move and burned every bridge behind him. He made no allowance for "saving face" or returning if his plans did not work out. In doing this he incurred the wrath of Pharaoh, but even that did not daunt him. He was "unawed and undismayed by the wrath of the king" (Hebrews 11:27, *Amplified*).

Pharaoh used every tactic to dissuade him from taking the Israelites to Canaan. At first he tried to break up his plan by offering several compromises. He suggested that if their purpose was to worship God there was no need to bother moving. He offered them religious liberty right there in Egypt (Exodus 8:25). When Moses declared that God wanted them to leave Egypt, Pharaoh made another suggestion. He proposed that they just go a short distance over the border (v. 28). Again that idea was rejected. It was not only necessary that they leave Egypt but also that they enter Canaan.

The next compromise was that only the men go to Canaan and the women and families be left behind (10:11). Even logic called for a rejection of that one. How long would the men stay away from their families? Finally, Pharaoh proposed that their possessions should remain (v. 24). Moses emphatically declared: "Not a hoof [shall] be left behind" (v. 26). Then he said a permanent goodbye to Pharaoh (v. 29) and by faith set out on a role of leadership that would bring God's people to their ancient homeland.

In his renunciation of Egypt, Moses is a noble example to us. There comes a time when we resolve to abandon the old haunts of sin and bid a firm farewell to the things that were such an integral part of our past life. Only by faith can we do as Moses did.

Enduring is not a pleasant experience. One of today's popular fallacies is that when one is in the will of God all will go smoothly. Nothing is farther from the truth. Moses had responded to the call of God and was in His perfect will. In spite of that, he faced almost insurmountable obstacles—enemies from among the heathen as well as criticism and rebellion from within. Someone has said that if Moses had been subjected to an annual election during his leadership of Israel he would have been voted out the first year. In spite of all these unpleasant experiences he remained firm in his intent and purpose.

There is a basic reason why Moses was willing and able to undergo such hardships. We are told: "He endured, as seeing him who is invisible." How do you see someone who is invisible? Only by faith. And that is the secret to Moses' remarkable achievements. Martin Luther's version says: "He held on to him whom he saw not, as though he saw him." Phillips' translation expresses it succinctly: "For he looked steadily at the ultimate, not the immediate, reward." By faith he was able to bear up under the sufferings and misfortunes that were his lot.

By faith we are also able to endure instead of succumbing to the swirling forces of this sinful world. The apostle James said: "Blessed is the man that endureth temptation" (James 1:12). As our eyes are fixed by faith on the Saviour, we become triumphantly victorious over that which would ordinarily destroy us. That was the secret for Moses and it is for us.

The five steps involved in Moses' historic choice are basic to all decisions we must make. We too are called to refuse, choose, esteem, forsake, and endure. With faith in our great Saviour we can triumph as he did.

14

Seeing the Plan of Redemption

> Through faith he kept the passover, and the sprinkling of blood, lest he that destroyed the firstborn should touch them.
>
> Hebrews 11:28

The Passover was the first and most important of the three annual festivals of Israel. It has a dual significance—historical and typical. Originally it was a supernatural deliverance from bondage and death (Exodus 12:27). It also foreshadows a much greater emancipation wrought by Jesus Christ (1 Corinthians 5:7).

The Passover was, and is, to Israel what the Lord's Supper is to the Christian. The two are intimately linked together. It was during the celebration of the Passover that Jesus instituted His commemorative supper. Both involved shed blood to procure life and liberty. The Christian sees salvation set forth in prospect by the Passover and in retrospect by the Lord's Supper.

The role of Moses in inaugurating the Passover is cited as being a magnificent example of faith: "By faith (simple trust and confidence in God) he instituted and carried out the Passover" *(Amplified)*. The element of faith was very strong in what he did. The plan was not his but God's. Even the most fertile human mind could not have produced a design for deliverance that would so intricately typify the freeing of all mankind from the plague of death.

When the plan was divulged to him he sensed something in it that would not have bcen perceived by an ordinary person. Cold logic and sheer reasoning would have looked on the scheme as ludicrous. By faith, however, he accepted God's plan and entered wholeheartedly into directing it, at the expense of making himself look ridiculous. Faith takes God at His Word and ventures forth, whatever the prospects of personal chagrin or embarrassment.

Not only did Moses institute the Passover, but he spearheaded the annual celebration as long as he lived. You can commemorate a historical event without a spark of faith in your heart, but that was not true in this instance. Moses looked not only to the past but to the future as well. He not only remembered what God had done for Israel but perceived what He would do for all mankind through the blood of the Lamb of God. As he had done in another exploit of faith, he acted while "seeing him who is invisible." A great faith accepted God's plan for the present and had insight into His better plan for the future.

No other creature could so beautifully typify Christ as the sacrificial lamb, especially since it had to be a perfect specimen with no blemishes. John introduced him by saying: "Behold the Lamb of God" (John 1:29). He was the Lamb God had provided. He was the antitype of all the lambs that had ever been sacrificed for man's sin, including the paschal lamb. He could be termed a lamb because He was innocent, sinless, spotless, and pure.

At the time of the Passover the lamb was an innocent victim, and so was Christ. The lamb became a substitute and died so the choice son of the household could live. Jesus Christ, in the plan of God, provided a substitutional atonement that "whosoever believeth in him should not perish, but have everlasting life" (3:16).

It was the blood of the lamb that was the key to the Passover. God said: "When I see the blood, I will pass over you" (Exodus 12:13). In like manner, the blood of Christ is the vital factor in delivering us from the presence and power of sin. Peter graphically reminds us of that fact: "Ye were . . . redeemed . . . with the precious blood of Christ, as of a lamb without blemish and without spot" (1 Peter 1:18, 19). The writer to the Hebrews stresses that truth also: "For if the blood of bulls and of goats, and the ashes of a heifer sprinkling the unclean, sanctifieth to the purifying of the flesh; how much more shall the blood of Christ, who through the eternal Spirit offered himself without spot to God, purge your conscience from dead works to serve the living God?" (Hebrews 9:13, 14).

Blood must be shed for redemption (v. 22). But the fact that it is thus spilled is not in itself sufficient. That blood must be applied. The Israelites were instructed to use hyssop and apply the blood to the lintel and doorposts of the home. It is a tremendous truth that Christ died for the sins of the whole world (1 John 2:2). In spite of that, many are not recipients of this blessing because the Blood has not been applied to their hearts by faith. It is those who receive Him and His sacrifice who become children of God and joint-heirs with Christ (John 1:12).

There are two interesting similarities in the ancient Passover and the blood atonement of Christ. Explicit instructions were given to the Israelites that no bones of the lamb were to be broken (Exodus 12:46). It is more than a coincidence that the Scriptures were fulfilled (Psalm 34:20) and no bones of Christ were broken (John 19:36). The other fascinating comparison is that although the blood was to be applied to the top and sides of the door, none was to be put on the threshold. Even in symbol and type no one was to tread on the blood of the covenant (Hebrews 10:28, 29).

The plan for a blood-bought atonement did not originate with man but in the mind of God himself. The whole plan of redemption is contrary to the thinking of the natural man. Those who approach religion through the exclusive avenue of reasoning speak disparagingly of such beliefs as "slaughterhouse religion." They claim the whole idea is repugnant to the aesthetic tastes of man. With a flippant attitude they discard the whole plan of blood atonement and proceed to build a philosophy on the life of Christ rather than on His death.

Faith supersedes reason in scriptural matters like these. It was faith that enabled Moses to accept the plan of the Lord; to see in it redemption; and to be willing to institute the Passover, direct its annual commemoration, and become the butt of abuse and ridicule by being closely affiliated with it. Although this action did not bring him the applause of men, it brought him into God's great hall of fame as an exponent of faith.

15
Faith or Presumption?

By faith they passed through the Red sea, as by dry land: which the Egyptians assaying to do were drowned.

Hebrews 11:29

A geographical name often takes on varied meanings to different people. To the English, Waterloo is synonymous with a surprising victory; but a French citizen equates it with defeat. Pearl Harbor means one thing to the Japanese and quite another to Americans. To the Israelites, even the thought of the Red Sea triggered great joy and rejoicing because of the victory God had wrought for them there. To the ancient Egyptians that body of water spoke of calamity and catastrophe when they lost their king and their entire army.

There is a right and a wrong way to do anything. Even when the objectives are identical, methods to accomplish them vary greatly. Some plans are successful and others are not. Some efforts are efficient and others are much less so. Such is the case in the Red Sea incident as recorded in Exodus 14:21-31.

Two human leaders wanted to get their followers to the other side of the Red Sea. They had that one objective in common. Moses and the unwieldy mass of humanity that was Israel had started for the land of promise. To get there they must cross that sea. Pharaoh, with his well-disciplined army, traveled that same route in pursuit of the slaves they had lost. Because Israel had crossed the sea, they must do so to overtake them. They had that selfsame geographical goal, but there the similarity ceases.

How basically different were these two efforts to cross the Red Sea! One was a success and the other was a failure. To the Israelites the task appeared difficult, if not impossible, and yet they crossed dry-shod. The Egyptians saw an open path and assumed it was easy. Their assessment proved to be faulty and disastrous. One decision was made by faith and the other was prompted by sight and based on presumption. One group ventured in obedience to the command of God while the other moved in defiance of His revealed plan. One was a triumph because of faith and the other was a catastrophe because of presumption.

Out of the Red Sea experience comes some practical and helpful lessons for us in our Christian life. We too tend to appraise situations by what we see and then determine our actions without reckoning on God. A faith that lays hold on the promises of God and moves in obedience to His command produces a victory that never comes through mere observation and reasoning.

Circumstances alone do not determine the will of God. How easy it is to assume that an open door indicates God's will and a closed one, the contrary. If that were the magic formula it would be unnecessary to seek God in determining His plan for our lives. Instead of getting the message from Him it would come from the kaleidoscopic pattern of earthly events, whimsical fate, and the result of man's ingenuity and labors. Is it plausible to look away from God to understand His thinking? That is as incredible as believing you can know the future by the chance location of tea leaves in the bottom of a cup.

If ever a door was closed it was when the Israelites were halted at the Red Sea. How easy it would have been to reason that they were out of God's will because they were confronted with an insurmountable obstacle. When they saw the enemy approaching from the rear they vented their feelings of having walked into a trap (14:10-12). Every visible evidence indicated that someone had made a mistake and they were out of God's will. Instead, they were right where God wanted them to be. All this happened so they might learn to receive their directions from the Lord and not from circumstances.

The experience of the Egyptians was the opposite. Just before they reached the sea God performed a miracle and there was a dry path right through the water. It is unlikely that Pharaoh ever gave consideration to the will of God, but had he done so he could have reasoned like some of us do at times. I can imagine him saying: "Isn't this wonderful. It must be God's will that I capture these Israelites. Here is an open path through the sea. God has given me an open door to do what I want to do." Such reasoning may seem plausible under the circumstances but it was all wrong.

Moses was confronted by a closed door and still he was in God's will. Pharaoh had an open door before him and yet it brought him headlong to his own destruction. It is very evident that circumstances alone do not determine God's will.

No one can get by on the faith of others. The experience of Pharaoh is a grim reminder of that fact. Any attempt to do so is sheer presumption and can lead to nothing but calamity. God opened the sea because Moses acknowledged Him, called upon Him, obeyed His command, and dared to venture by faith in Him. Such faith moves the arm of God. Pharaoh and his hordes audaciously assumed they could squeeze through while the door was open. The ghastly sight of human bodies strewn along the beach (v. 30) emphasized the folly of his action. God merely lifted His hand and the waters took their natural course. Pharaoh only fooled himself and brought about his own destruction. Salvation for the man of faith meant condemnation for the man of presumption.

The arrogance that made Pharaoh presume on the grace of God was not limited to him or to his age. In all generations men have done the same, to their own destruction. Children attempt to hitchhike to heaven on the faith of a godly parent. The unbeliever in a Christian household clings to a feeble hope that enough faith and righteousness will spill over onto him to enable him to get into the pearly gates, in spite of his defiance of God's will and plan. Some have the affrontery to assert boldly that God cannot do otherwise than admit them to heaven. Wishful thinking makes them demand such access. These reasonings are based on presumption instead of faith. No person has ever been granted entrance into heaven on the faith of another—and none ever will.

Faith in a great God solves great problems. The greatness of faith itself is not of paramount importance. It is not whether our faith is sufficient for the problem but whether God is. We have no gauge by which to measure faith. If an impasse calls for gigantic faith, there may be a question as to whether ours is adequate. However, if we have faith in an all-sufficient God, then we have reason to rejoice.

Jesus said that if we have faith the size of a mustard seed we can move mountains (Matthew 17:20). Too often we assume that if we have faith the size of a mountain we can move a mustard seed. If the solution depends on the size of our faith we may rightly waver, but if it depends on the size of our God then we can expect victory. Whatever the size or quality of Moses' faith, we do not know. He had faith in a God who could do the impossible and so he led his people toward the water in obedience to God's command.

Presumption bases its conclusions on observation, circumstances, and human reasoning. Faith reckons on the God who is greater than all of these. At the Red Sea Pharaoh demonstrated one and Moses the other.

16

Strange Strategy

> By faith the walls of Jericho fell down, after they were compassed about seven days.
>
> Hebrews 11:30

Never in the history of warfare were such ludicrous military tactics used as those employed in the ancient battle of Jericho. This motley mob of slaves had no trained army, no military experience, and no traditional weapons to attack a walled city. In spite of these limitations and their illogical strategy, Jericho stands out as one of the greatest of all victories for the Israelites. How could this be? The divine writer reminds us that it was only by faith that it could and did happen.

Jericho was a sun-drenched, walled fortress located on a rich plain in the Jordan Valley, about 7 miles north of the Dead Sea. It was situated in a magnificent forest of palm trees some 8 miles long and 3 miles broad. Because of that it was often called "The City of Palms" (Deuteronomy 34:3; Judges 1:16; 2 Chronicles 28:15).

It was renowned for its wealth, commerce, and luxury. The gates were strong and well guarded. The walls were sturdy with many houses on top of them

(Joshua 2:15). In natural reasoning the city was veritably impregnable. It had stood for years and in all likelihood would continue for decades or centuries. Jericho was prepared for any concerted onslaught except that of faith.

Just why would Joshua and his hordes attack such a fortified city as their initial venture in the land of promise? They did so not only because this was God's plan for them but for very logical reasons as well. The storied reply of a mountain climber when asked why he wants to climb a certain peak is, "Because it is there." Jericho was right in their path and that was a valid reason for their beginning there. Had they bypassed that formidable obstacle they would have always been subject to attack from the rear. That is an untenable position in any military endeavor.

We could well learn two basic steps to success by following the example of the Israelites in this instance. The first principle is to confront every obstacle as it comes. Avoiding a decision or a battle only makes matters more difficult. If we are to be at all selective we should do what they did—tackle the hardest task first. These two precepts contribute much to making any person a victorious overcomer.

The city of Jericho was the first formidable object in the Israelites' path and it called for their initial conflict with an enemy. We can visualize Joshua furtively approaching the walls of that city and, in the glistening moonlight, surveying the fortress. He was privately reconnoitering; sketching his strategy and maneuvers. His mind was engrossed in the problems of the battle. He walked around the city, thinking his own thoughts, making his own plans, and wondering how best to capture it.

Suddenly Joshua realized he was not alone. An

armed figure was towering over him with a drawn sword. It was surprising to meet anyone in that lonely place, but especially someone with a sword in hand. Soldier that he was, Joshua would not be intimidated. He challenged the stranger, "Are you friend or foe?" That was a natural question to be asked of an armed man in an enemy country. It left no room for neutrality but called for a clear-cut declaration of allegiance.

The answer greatly surprised Joshua. The stranger declared he was the Commander of the Lord's host. What did he mean? Which was the Lord's army? Certainly it was not the heathen enemy. It could only mean the Israelites—God's people. Further, He said He was the *Commander* of that army. Was that not the very position Joshua had recently assumed? Who was this who was laying claim to his position?

It was no imposter, but the Lord himself. Joshua was aware of a divine visitation. God had appeared similarly to his forebears, Abraham and Jacob, and also to Moses. This time there was no dream, vision, or burning bush, but the Lord came to a gallant warrior in the guise of a human fighting man with a drawn sword. Here on the border of the Promised Land, the first Joshua met the second Joshua, our Saviour. He who was the type met the antitype and it all happened in God's plan.

The attitude of Joshua was noble and exemplary. He removed his shoes, which was the same token of respect that Moses gave at the burning bush. He bowed in worship and then waited for orders from the One who was his superior. By that act he acknowledged that he was but second-in-command. He had come face-to-face with the Commander-in-Chief of the Lord's army. While waiting in His presence, Joshua received the full plan for the forthcoming conflict (Joshua 6:1-5). Then together they executed the strange strategy of the battle of Jericho and the result was a glorious victory.

Joshua had implicit faith in God and was confident that he had met with Him in that moonlight conference. That faith caused him to abandon his own military plans and to put himself and his men completely at the disposal of the One who was his superior. Faith was the motivating force that brought about unconditional obedience. It mattered not whether the battle plan was a tried and proven one or absurd and unreasonable. As far as he was concerned, it was not what the strategy was that was important, but *whose* it was. If the plan originated with the Lord, then by faith in Him he would carry it out.

The congregation also responded by faith. It took a great faith to go along with a plan that, even to a layman, appeared to be sheer folly. Who would risk his life and become the object of ridicule by just marching around a wall? Still, there was no uprising when the tactics were presented to them. They too had faith in a great God and if it was His plan then they had every confidence it would work.

The decisions came from the Commander-in-Chief, and Joshua and the people acted in faith and merely carried out His orders. They did what they were told and left the rest to God. Obedience doesn't ask how or why the victory will come, but leaves that to the One who is directing the battle.

The battle plan would have brought guffaws of laughter from experienced military tacticians. Seven priests headed a procession, blowing ram's horn trumpets. Then came the ark of the covenant and the people followed in absolute silence. They circled the entire city once a day for 6 days. Then on the 7th day they compassed the city seven times, making a grand total of 13 trips. Seven such trips in one day would greatly weaken even the strongest warrior and make him less able to combat an enemy.

Why all this useless waste of energy and effort? By this time the residents of the city were gathered on the walls and heckling this riffraff army that was parading and apparently trying to put a hex on them. Common sense said this whole effort was utter folly.

But suddenly something happened! The seventh lap of the day was finished. The trumpets sounded again and this time the people shouted. Joshua declared: "The Lord hath given you the city." With that the walls crumbled and the surprised enemy took flight. God's people won their first major battle! The victory was sudden, sure, and complete. Surely, it was not because of the tactics. Such an approach was never used before or since. It was by faith in a great God that the victory came.

God deigns to use human instruments in working His miracles. He could effect His plan without visible means, but He chooses to do otherwise. In this instance and in many others, the contrast between apparently illogical means and the dramatic results is very great. He incorporated the efforts of men into His preannounced plan and purpose. The means He used did not originate with men, but He prescribed them himself.

The Israelites' part was merely to follow God's instructions. Even in looking back on the action there is no evident connection between the means used and the results that followed. In that circumstance, why were means essential to the plan? Why the daily march and the final shout of the people? Couldn't such efforts have been eliminated and the walls made to fall while the expectant Israelites just looked on? Not even the wildest flight of imagination could conclude that sturdy walls would collapse because of tramping feet, seven trumpet blasts, and the shout of thousands of people. Yet, it was only *after* the walls were compassed that they fell. That word *after* is significant. As men respond to God's plan, whatever the details may be, they become partners with God in producing a miracle.

The contrast between the irrelevant means used by men and the dramatic victory that followed points up God's power in the whole matter. No one would ever claim the triumph came because of human strategy or efforts. And yet, the results came only *after* man did his feeble part. It all leads back to the supernatural element of faith.

There is no area of life in which faith cannot enter and make an integral contribution to victory. The textbooks of military academies make no allowance for faith, but the experience in this ancient battle reminds us that it has and can make the difference between defeat and victory.

17
The Faith of a Sinner

> By faith the harlot Rahab perished not with them that believed not, when she had received the spies with peace.
>
> Hebrews 11:31

There are many surprises in God's gallery of faith. One involves the instances in any given life that are selected as examples of faith. Were we to choose such instances our choices would differ greatly from those given in this superb faith chapter. We are also surprised at some of the persons included in this list of giants of faith. One person we would be apt to overlook is Rahab, the heathen harlot. Yet, her name is listed with the patriarchs and those who shine because of their exploits of faith.

Rahab was a most unlikely prospect for the faith "hall of fame." There was nothing conducive to faith in her early life in heathen Jericho. Her means of making a livelihood brought reproach, rather than esteem, from her fellow citizens. Her occupation became a part of her identity. When she is mentioned in the Books of Joshua, Hebrews, and James she is called, "Rahab the harlot."

Some have rationalized that perhaps she was merely an innkeeper, but a careful study of the record indicates otherwise. Her job was most likely a combination of both activities. Her life was tarnished by idolatry and adultery. In a list of those cited for exemplary living, noble activities, or religious purity, Rahab would never have been considered. But here she is among the great examples of those who demonstrated real faith. To some this is indeed shocking, but to others it is a brilliant example of the grace of God.

Perhaps the best description of her life was given by M. A. Martin, a preacher of a previous century:

> Think what a moral mixture the human heart may hold, what a mass of contradictions it is! Rahab the loyal lover to her kindred, traitor to her king, gifted with insight above her fellow citizens, yet exposing herself, possessed of a crude faith, yet selling her honor for gain! Surely the warp of heaven and the woof of hell were never woven together more strangely. Surely there never was such a peculiar character thrown off from the loom of life.

This woman of great faith was an Amorite and hence a Gentile. She had no religious background and lived among those who knew nothing about Jehovah. Her means of knowledge was very limited and natural events would have tended to swallow her up in the mass of heathenism. Out of such a strange background rises a towering faith that is most singular and unique.

One of the surprising aspects about Rahab is that she became an ancestress of Jesus (Matthew 1:5). The combination of her faith and the grace of God transformed this disreputable pariah into one who would be admired and respected by succeeding generations. She was not the only person with a defiled past in the lineage of our Lord. Also included were incestuous Tamar, idolatrous Ruth, and adulterous Bathsheba. While man tends to remember the stains and vileness, the grace of God surmounts them and causes us to stand in wonderment. Jesus astonished the chief priests by saying: "Verily I say unto you, That the publicans and the harlots go into the kingdom of God before you" (21:31).

Just how did that spark of faith come into the life of Rahab? How is that little seed planted in any heart? The apostle Paul writes: "So then faith cometh by hearing, and hearing by the word of God" (Romans 10:17). That sounds so simple to us but it was not so to her. There were no Scriptures available to Rahab. The voice of no prophet rang out on the streets of Jericho and no neighbors put forth efforts to tell her of Jehovah.

Faith did not come to her by hearing God's Word, but she did hear of His works. She heard of the miracles God had wrought and the victories by His power (Joshua 2:10, 11). This brought her to logical conclusions and a bold declaration: "The Lord your God, he is God in heaven above, and in earth beneath." By His works she judged Him to be God indeed.

After her acceptance of Jehovah as her God, Rahab wisely moved into step with Him. She sensed what He was doing and yielded to His plan. She made her life to conform to His purpose. She sensed that the judgment of God would come to her city and that she must do something to escape it. Faith brought about action on her part. Real faith always produces works. The writer of this Epistle and James do not contradict one another (Hebrews 11:31; James 2:25). Faith produces works and they are always coupled together.

The faith of Rahab was not only personal but it was also household faith. It was an umbrella that covered her parents, her brethren, and all of her family. Each individual benefited because of her faith in Jehovah (Joshua 6:23). The red cord, like the blood on the doorposts in Egypt, provided protection for all within the house. All in its confines were spared, while all outside were destroyed. An entire family was spared by the faith of one. Anyone else in Jericho had the same opportunity to hear, believe, and act but no one else did so. This made the faith of Rahab outstanding.

Some purists have raised their eyebrows at certain events in the experience of Rahab. It must be conceded that there are puzzling aspects in this incident that confound us all. Some have questioned the propriety of the men of Israel staying in the home of a harlot. As previously mentioned, however, that home was most likely the local inn and the logical place for strangers to lodge.

The biggest problem has to do with the lie Rahab told, prompted by the good motive of saving the lives of the Israelites (2:4, 5). Is such a lie ever justified? Are such tactics a part of God's plan in preserving His own? If Rahab was such a noble example of faith why would she be guilty of this moral turpitude? Did God encourage, smile upon, or justify in any way such prevarication?

We tend to think of these persons as being perfect just because they exemplified unusual faith. Such is not the case. Perhaps it takes such a glaring failure as Rahab's life to remind us that there is no attempt to present these heroes of faith as sinless, but to highlight the quality of faith in their lives. Faith in God produces morality but it isn't always spontaneous.

The forging of a lie and reliance upon it must have been a carryover from her past life. Surely God didn't instruct her to do that. He has ways of working without that universal tool of sin, but she had done things like that so often in the past it seemed second nature to do so. We should greatly admire the faith of Rahab, but not follow her example in all things.

Faith envisioned God's plan for the future and directed Rahab to be in the right place at the right time and with the right attitude of submission to God. Such a faith led from a sordid past into the royal line of the Messiah and then to the hall of fame in the Bible.

18

Heroes Unlimited

And what shall I more say? for time would fail me to tell of Gideon, and of Barak, and of Samson, and of Jephthah; and of David also, and Samuel and of the prophets: who through faith subdued kingdoms, wrought righteousness, obtained promises, stopped the mouths of lions, quenched the violence of fire, escaped the edge of the sword, out of weakness were made strong, waxed valiant in fight, turned to flight the armies of the aliens.

Women received their dead raised to life again: and others were tortured, not accepting deliverance; that they might obtain a better resurrection: and others had trial of cruel mockings and scourgings, yea, moreover of bonds and imprisonment; they were stoned, they were sawn asunder, were tempted, were slain with the sword: they wandered about in sheepskins and goatskins; being destitute, afflicted, tormented; of whom the world was not worthy: they wandered in deserts, and in mountains, and in dens and caves of the earth.

And these all, having obtained a good report through faith, received not the promise: God having provided some better thing for us, that they without us should not be made perfect.

Hebrews 11:32-40

As this great faith chapter draws to a close the writer rises to lofty heights of eloquence. With a burst of rhetoric he launches into the most glowing passage in the entire Epistle. Using crisp, colorful words he paints a vivid picture of unusual exploits of faith and extends the list of its unheralded champions. Their names may not be as prominent as the previous ones but the individuals were no less giants of faith.

The most important truth in this passage is that the honor roll of faith is not complete. The last name will not be inscribed there until faith is forever changed to sight. The limitations of time and space made it impossible for the apostle Paul to complete the list of even those in the Old Testament era. Who could give a detailed record of the exploits and examples of faith since the birth of the Church on the Day of Pentecost? Daring and venturesome faith is being demonstrated in our own age and some of our contemporaries qualify for that great honor society. Hebrews 11 merely gives us a fleeting glimpse into the chronicles of faith. Only in the annals of heaven will the record be complete.

The six men named here rose from humble beginnings to places of leadership among their people. Four of them were judges of Israel, one was a king, and the other (Samuel) was the first of the prophets. Their backgrounds were anything but royal or noble. Gideon was a farmer, David a shepherd, Barak a soldier, Samson a religious Nazirite, and Jephthah had somewhat of a questionable birth. Yet, they found common ground in that all were men of great faith in God.

Some Bible scholars have been puzzled that these men are not listed in chronological order. That is of little significance and bears no importance to the matter at hand. The key is that imperfect men of modest origins rose to great heights because of their faith and are held forth to all of us as magnificent examples. Many others are equally outstanding but their names are not mentioned. In climaxing this great chapter the writer presents valiant names, then valiant deeds, and, finally, valiant endurance. All of these were made possible by faith.

The experiences of these worthies were diversified and varied but one background was common to them all. It is summed up in the phrase: "Out of weakness were made strong" (v. 34). It is out of the soil of human weakness that faith grows. When a man senses his own frailty and impotence he reaches out to lay hold on a mighty God. Faith is the means by which such action is accomplished. Whether it be conquering nations, withstanding savage animals, or suffering martyrdom, faith enables him to rise from the shambles of human weakness to the majestic heights of heroic accomplishments.

A humble awareness of one's own weakness lays the groundwork for great exploits of faith. When someone asked Hudson Taylor to give the reason for his great missionary accomplishments he uttered the classic statement: "The Lord was looking for a man weak enough to use and he found me."

What is recorded in this illustrious chapter of the Bible is written for our encouragement and inspiration. Nothing is more heartening to us than this truth that faith came out of weakness. We readily identify with men of weakness and are inspired to exercise such faith as has been implanted in our hearts and to honor God by venturing forth on His promises. If by faith they could rise above the ordinary and become outstanding in God's eyes, then we can do the same.

The exceptional courage of many of these noble ones is evidenced in verse 35: "And others were tortured, not accepting deliverance." They had the option of going free but deliberately chose not to do so. Without a doubt, the opportunity carried with it the necessity to compromise and not even temporary freedom was worth that price. With the alternatives of extended suffering or concession to evil, they chose the former. Faith evaluates present, temporary benefits as opposed to eternal rewards and accepts suffering in the place of tainted freedom.

How vastly different are the appraisals made by God and man. Nothing points out that sharp contrast more than this passage. Men counted these individuals as the outcasts of the earth and expendable. From the vantage point of heaven, however, they were viewed as the elite of the human family. Those who were rejected by men were accepted by God. They were "spurned and ill-treated by a world that was too evil to see their worth" (v. 38, *Phillips*). Actually, they were too good for this world. It was not innate human qualities or abilities that set them apart, but a faith that lifted them toward God. It alone enabled them to lay hold on eternal principles and react accordingly. Such a faith made their actions different from those of ordinary men and secured for them God's smile of approval.

We must be continually reminded of one fact: The strength or value of faith is not to be judged by the immediate, visible results. In summation of this the writer says: "And these all . . . received not the promise." That is somewhat of a repetition of what he wrote in verse 13: "These all died in faith, not having received the promises." By the end of their lives they did not see literally accomplished what their faith had anticipated. The casual observer would conclude that the results of their faith were limited and incomplete. Some would question whether it was actually real faith.

Here, again, God's evaluation and conclusions are at variance with ours. These men of faith entered into God's thinking and anticipated long-range results in spite of the approach of death and the lack of corroborating evidence. In that sense, faith is the evidence of things not seen. Although these persons lived long before us they will eventually share with us the realities that faith embraced: "For God wanted them to wait and share the even better rewards that were prepared for us" (v. 40, *The Living Bible*).

Every person listed or alluded to in this gallery of the gallant is there because of his faith. Each one had a faith that was tested severely. No two experiences were alike nor were the testings born of similar circumstances or of the same intensity. Faith that is tried becomes a viable faith. Peter reminds us that the *trial* of our faith is most valuable: "The trial of your faith, being much more precious than . . . gold" (1 Peter 1:7). That which we shy from is that which develops us into giants of faith.

This faith chapter concludes, but the exploits of faith continue to be written in the records of heaven.